SORTING LETTERS ON THE SEA

Holyhead mail boats and the *Leinster* tragedy

Stephen Ferguson

Foreword

I swim in the Forty Foot bathing hole on the edge of Dublin Bay every Saturday morning. It is a tranquil spot for locals to chat and have a dip. The shape of the little cove focuses the eye on the horizon by the Kish bank 8kms offshore.

It was in the Forty Foot that I first learnt of the tragedy of postal workers on the mailboat the RMS *Leinster*, torpedoed by a German U-boat by the Kish Bank. One of the two torpedoes was a direct hit on the ship's post office. 21 of the 22 workers on that shift were killed. The *Leinster* was the greatest tragedy of either World War on Irish soil or in Irish waters. 500 were killed as the *Leinster* sank rapidly. Some were rescued and made it to shore.

Several regulars at the Forty Foot are direct descendants or related to those who drowned. They tell stories of their mothers or fathers walking the pier in Dun Laoghaire, from where the mailboat sailed, out of habit to remember uncles or aunts drowned on the *Leinster*. For An Post it is especially poignant. Our postal staff would have travelled out that morning from central Dublin, most from the North Inner City, to sort the day's mail bound for London. The boat was the fastest ever (to this day, other than catamarans) to cross the Irish Sea and had to leave right on time so the mail could be in London, sorted, by that evening for delivery the next day.

We all know from history that the First World War ended on the 11th hour of the 11th day of the 11th month in 1918. The tragedy of the RMS *Leinster* is that it was sunk on the 10th hour of the 10th day of the 10th month of 1918, so close to the end of the war. The terrible loss of life was so close to war's end, that it became forgotten, almost erased from history as the world moved forward. I grew up in Dublin, in Dundrum, and knew almost nothing of the *Leinster* (there is the *Leinster's* anchor on the promenade in Dun Laoghaire but no one paid much notice). I never knew of the fate of the postal workers.

So this centenary is the time to remember and honour all who died and particularly our colleagues killed that morning. An Post will be marking the event in various

ways and taking part in the State's commemoration on the anniversary. Stephen Ferguson's book sets the story of the *Leinster* in the particular context of the Post Office and the Holyhead mail boats: all who walk Dun Laoghaire pier or look out to sea from the Forty Foot will appreciate the light it sheds on a national tragedy that has remained too long in the shadows.

From 1811 until 1965 a lightship was moored on the sandy shallows of the Kish bank to give warning to sailors. A lighthouse now serves the same purpose. (An Post Museum & Archive)

David McRedmond
Chief Executive
An Post

Contents

Opposite page: Elegant, punctual and very fast, the *Leinster* was all that a Royal Mail Steamer should be. The turtle-back deck at the bow allowed it to plough through heavy seas and afforded protection for mail bags stowed beneath its roof. (Davisonphoto/Chapman Livingston Collection)

Preface

In an age where many people enjoy the benefits of virtually instant communication, it is difficult to appreciate now the role of the Post Office a century and more ago. It was the communications giant of its day and the humble letter was the instrument that facilitated commerce, united families and kept the wheels of Government in motion. The electric telegraph and the telephone were available a hundred years ago certainly – both again in the hands of the Post Office – but they were comparatively expensive and their use, for most people, was restricted to emergencies and special occasions. The letter was cheap: the penny postal rate, made famous through the world's first adhesive postage stamp, the Penny Black, had remained unchanged from 1840 until June 1915, when the pressures of a wartime economy forced the Government to raise the rate to a penny halfpenny. In the public mind, the Post Office was the friendly face of Government and postmen, clerks and telegraphists were the respected agents of an institution which existed to serve the public good.

For Irishmen and women who wanted to keep in touch with those who had left the country to seek better lives elsewhere, for businessmen with contacts throughout the rest of the United Kingdom and for the politicians and civil servants in Dublin and London who sought to steer a course through the choppy waters of Anglo-Irish relations, the mail boats that plied the Irish Sea route between Kingstown (Dún Laoghaire) and Holyhead were the high speed broadband of their time. A mail boat or "packet" ship, as it continued to be called in the Post Office years after the term had been dropped from ordinary use, had been a feature of Irish communication since Elizabethan times.

Boats crossed the Irish Sea not just from Dublin but from several harbours along the east coast – Donaghadee, Belfast, Dunmore and Waterford, for instance. In the days of sail, the passage was entirely dependent on the weather and the postal service was irregular with several different letter dispatches and newspapers often arriving together. The advent of steam ships heralded a new dawn in speed and regularity. The early days of steam, however, were not always pleasant for the passengers with nauseous fumes a frequent cause of complaint but by the mid-nineteenth century,

technology had improved and, while the Irish Sea could always be a rough crossing, passenger numbers had increased and shipping companies were doing good business. Foremost amongst these was the City of Dublin Steam Packet Company.

For eighty years this Company was closely associated with the Irish Post Office and its commercial success owed much to the skill with which, for seventy years, it held on to the valuable mail contract for the Kingstown-Holyhead route. Its mail boats, which carried the designation RMS for Royal Mail Steamer, were very fast, reliable and stylish, their reputation extending far beyond the shores of the Irish Sea. The RMS title was first used by the Post Office in 1840 in connection with Samuel Cunard's contract to carry mail between Liverpool and North America and many famous ships, not least the *Titanic* and the *Lusitania*, have since proudly used the term. When the RMS *Leinster*, with great loss of life, was torpedoed just a few weeks before the end of the First World War, it was a national tragedy and would presage the end of a remarkable tradition of service and co-operation between the Company and the

The City of Dublin Steam Packet Company produced several postcard designs to advertise its services. This one of the *Leinster*, viewed through a porthole, is particularly effective. (An Post Museum & Archive)

Post Office. Circumstances would combine to obscure the memory of the disaster in the public mind and it is fitting now, a century after the *Leinster* was lost, that the events of that time should be brought to mind again. Amongst those who perished on that tragic October day were twenty-one of the twenty-two Post Office staff who manned the ship's sorting office. This is the particular story of the work they did and of the ships that plied the Irish Sea maintaining that great chain of postal communication that ran from Dublin to London via Kingstown and Holyhead.

Stephen Ferguson
General Post Office Dublin

Early days

Lo. Here I sit at Holy Head
With muddy ale and mouldy bread,
I'm fastened both by wind and tide,
I see the ships at anchor ride …
The captain swears the sea too rough,
(he has not passengers enough).
And thus the Dean is forc'd to stay
Till others come to help the pay.

Attributed to Jonathan Swift

Jonathan Swift, priest, politician and patriot, was an Irishman who knew better than most the perils and pleasures of sailing between Ireland and Britain. In these few humorous lines we catch not only a glimpse of the great satirist whose pen gave us *Gulliver's Travels*, *A Modest Proposal* and the *Drapier's letters* but also an insight into the trials that faced all those whose business obliged them to undertake the sea journey between Dublin and Holyhead. Given the intimate political and economic connections that have always existed between Ireland and Britain the story of the maritime communication between the two islands is an important one. Separated at the narrowest point by just twelve miles, a disinterested observer would be forgiven for assuming that the Irish Sea passage, compared with the great distances involved in transatlantic, Indian or Australian routes, offers little of interest for the historian, postal or maritime. On the contrary, Ireland's status as England's oldest colony, the complex political relations between the two countries, their important trade ties and the constant flow of Irish people in search of employment, fame and fortune abroad, make the tale of packet ships and mail boats a vivid one. So deeply embedded within the Irish psyche is the notion of the mail boat as the vehicle of emigration – its twice daily departure from Dún Laoghaire to Holyhead a part of Dublin life until very recently – that many people entirely gloss over the word 'mail' and forget that these ships were, for generations, the principal means of maintaining all contact, personal and governmental, between these sister islands. A brisk walk down the east pier on a summer's evening with perhaps a "Teddy's 99" in your hand and the ambition of getting to the end before the *Hibernia* left the harbour was the ideal of relaxation for Dubliners who lived within hearing of the ships' sirens.

Opposite page: Packet boats, heading for Dublin in the early days of the service, were often glad to find safety in harbours anywhere between Arklow and Balbriggan. (Stephen Ferguson)

From the later Middle Ages, ships heading for Dublin landed where they could along the coast, with landfall made anywhere from Arklow in the south to Balbriggan in the north, with the small havens at Bullock and Dalkey offering protection and the possibility of onward transport by boat or on horseback to Dublin. Dublin Bay itself, until the detailed survey undertaken by Captain Bligh of *Bounty* fame in the winter of 1800, was known for its shifting sands and the Liffey bar, both of which made entrance to the city's port difficult. There is no complete record of the number of ships that have been wrecked in Dublin Bay but there were many – and packet ships foundered too. One ship, the mail packet *William*, was driven ashore near Sutton in 1694 with more than eighty aboard and only the master and the ship's boy survived on that occasion. *Faulkner's Dublin Journal* of 19 January 1745 states that Theophilus Cibber and other actors perished when the mail packet from Parkgate on the Wirral peninsula, a regular departure point for Ireland in the eighteenth century until the Dee silted up, was wrecked on the North Bull. A century later the *Tayleur*, a Royal Mail ship en route from Liverpool to Australia, ran aground on Lambay Island on its maiden voyage in 1854. The loss of some 380 lives on that occasion would remain the greatest loss of life in the Irish Sea until the *Leinster* tragedy. Sailing, in short, was perilous and the journey between Ireland and Britain was not something to be lightly undertaken.

It was the tiny settlement of Dunleary, some seven miles south-east of Dublin's city centre, which was destined to become the gateway for communication between Ireland and Britain. Old Dunleary had a small harbour – the outline survives as the inner pier

at the 'Coal Harbour' – and boatmen there used to earn money by rowing out to packet ships becalmed in the bay and waiting for a wind to get into Ringsend, Poolbeg or the Pigeon House. Dublin Bay was especially treacherous in certain conditions and the loss of some 400 people aboard the *Prince of Wales* and the *Rochdale* in November 1807 – more than a century before the *Leinster* disaster – concentrated attention on the need to provide better protection for those travelling to and from the capital. Even though a new harbour had recently been constructed for the Post Office at Howth, the case for a new 'asylum' harbour at Dunleary was compelling. When George IV visited Ireland in 1821, he found work on the new harbour in full swing and the old town of Dunleary was renamed Kingstown in his honour. An obelisk, just a few yards from where the anchor of the *Leinster* also rests, commemorates the occasion.[1] By 1848, when the harbour was more or less complete, Kingstown had taken over from Howth as the Post Office packet station with mail conveyed to the ships on the trains that ran daily from Westland Row station.

On the other side of the Irish Sea, Holyhead was the place which offered the closest contact with Dublin but it was very remote and inconvenient for wheeled transport so Chester was sometimes the departure point for travellers. The establishment of a formal mail boat between Ireland and Britain goes back to the time of Elizabeth I and occasional glimpses of this irregular and perilous service are found in the State Papers of the period. In 1561 Patrick Tirrell of Howth was contracted by Government to provide a boat while, on the other side of the Irish Sea, John Apperce of Holyhead was engaged to set up a service between the two countries.

Opposite page: Howth harbour was, in the early nineteenth century, the base for packets crossing the Irish Sea and milestones still mark the mail coach route from there to the GPO. Silt and the increasing size of mail boats led the Post Office to move business to Kingstown in January 1834. (Stephen Ferguson)

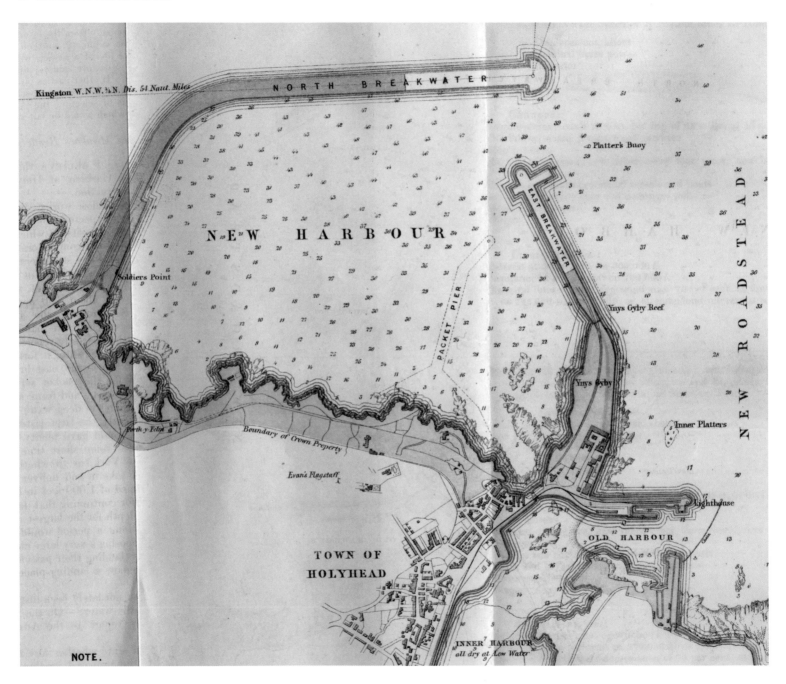

Kingston W.N.W. ¼ N. Dis. 54 Naut. Miles

NORTH BREAKWATER

NEW HARBOUR

EAST BREAKWATER

Platter's Buoy

NEW ROADSTEAD

Soldiers Point

Ynys Gyby Reef

PACKET PIER

Ynys Gyby

Inner Platters

Porth y Felin

Boundary of Crown Property

Evan's Flagstaff

Lighthouse

OLD HARBOUR

TOWN OF
HOLYHEAD

INNER HARBOUR
all dry at Low Water

NOTE.

Payments to Apperce and a William Tyrell of Clontarf are recorded for March 1568 with further expenses the following year of £4-19-6½ to Apperce and £3-10-0 to Patrick Tyrell.[2] Pirates based at Beaumaris in Anglesey posed dangers in these early days while in July 1631 it was claimed that the packet ship had fallen victim to pirates all the way from Turkey. A century and a half later, the *Bessborough* and *Hillsborough* packets fell victim to American privateers. Those who provided the boats had to contend not only with these dangers but also defend themselves against regular charges of delay. In a letter to the Earl of Salisbury, written at Howth on 4 April 1608, Sir Arthur Chichester, the Irish Lord Deputy, defended one Holyhead-based captain, Robert Pepper, against charges that Pepper's 'ordinary bark, used for transportation of letters or packets hither' was nothing but 'a baggage boat'. Chichester, on the contrary, praised Pepper and his little boat which, he said, 'passes to and fro like a light horseman'.[3] Kind words were welcome but getting paid was another matter. Pepper's successor, Andrew Hooper, was apparently reduced to such a state that he was forced to pawn his goods, leaving him with just the clothes on his back and his wife with a smock! Contemporary records refer to these little mail boats as ships 'with furniture to transport the packets to Ireland', a rather cumbersome formula, which gave way to the simpler "packet" boat. The term packet itself, of course, means a packet of letters, and the Post Office, in legal language, still refers to its rights and duties in respect of postal packets.

With wars added to the usual uncertainties of wind and weather, communication between the two islands remained throughout the seventeenth century a rather haphazard affair. In a letter of 23 April 1670, the Irish Lord Lieutenant wrote that 'There is general complaint in England and here of the delay of the packet boats … I have complained of this to Mr. Warburton [the postmaster], who has promised to make enquiry of the master of the boat.'[4] The more tranquil and prosperous eighteenth century allowed the mail boat service to settle down but with prosperity came increased costs. In 1705 for instance, James Vickers had conveyed the mails from Holyhead to Dublin for an annual sum of £600 but by 1742, when the contract was with John Power, the cost had risen to £900. In December 1767, the Deputy Postmaster for Ireland, William Fortescue, proposed a six-day service on the Irish Sea with three more vessels to be based at Holyhead. The cost was considerable – a total of £2,355 – but the Post Office was making profits and his proposal was duly implemented.

By the time legislation establishing an independent Irish Post Office was enacted in 1784, there were five vessels, of about seventy tons each, employed as packet ships under direct contract between the Postmaster General (PMG) and the respective commanders. They received £350 each year for conveyance of the mails but were also entitled to the profits arising from passenger and freight traffic as well. The *Bibliotheca Topographica Britannica* of 1793, in its entry for Holyhead, notes that, at that time, Thomas Blair, a Dublin merchant, was being paid £300 p.a. for the vessels he supplied to Government with £150 allowed 'for accidents', an interesting provision in the light of the fate that would befall the *Leinster* and other mail boats during the First World War. He had, in addition, 'all the benefit arising from the conveyance of passengers' to whom he charged half a guinea for a bed in a cabin and just half a crown for those who felt themselves content 'walking upon deck or in the hold'. By the close of the eighteenth century, the principle consequently had been well established that ship owners might successfully combine their public sector mail contract with lucrative private sector passenger business.

The Act of Union, which united the parliaments of Ireland and Britain in 1800, changed the nature of the political relationship between the two kingdoms. The importance of the Dublin-London connection and its influence on so many facets of the political, commercial and cultural relationship between the two countries is well summarised in this extract from an 1815 House of Commons report on the state of the Holyhead road:

> *The great and paramount duties of Legislation; the necessity of making applications and appeals from Ireland to the English Courts of Law … the carrying on of a trade exceeding twenty millions in annual value between England and Ireland; the extension of family connections between the inhabitants of both Countries; the general and beneficial practice among the better classes in Ireland of educating their children in England; and the speedy conveyance of the correspondence of the United Kingdom, are political objects of such great public consideration, as, in the opinion of Your Committee, fully to justify the most liberal aid being granted by Parliament, with a view of overcoming the obstructions to the attaining of them, which the present state of the Welsh Road interposes.* [5]

The attitude towards Ireland is a trifle condescending, perhaps, but the argument that the Dublin-London axis is of vital importance to the United Kingdom is made quite clear and by 1853 another House of Commons committee would confidently assert that, since the Union, the establishment and maintenance of the best and speediest means of communication between the two countries had been regarded as 'the paramount duty of Government'.[6] It fell to the great Scottish road builder, Thomas Telford, to make of the hills and valleys of north Wales a coach road that would help achieve the objects enunciated by the MPs in Westminster. His engineering genius in road and bridge building facilitated faster mail coach travel on the London to Holyhead route but it was the application of steam power, both to railways and ships, which really transformed communication between Ireland and Britain and contributed to the greatly increased importance of the Post Office over the next century.

Private commercial interests had been quick to see the potential of steam on the Irish Sea: a steamship had visited Howth in 1816 and, in July 1819, the steamship *Talbot* began carrying passengers to Holyhead during the summer. The businessmen behind the new venture approached the GPO and offered to carry the mails, firstly for £1,000 and subsequently free, but the Post Office indignantly rejected the overture, arguing that 'to entrust any part of a service of such importance to private individuals was highly objectionable in principle'.[7] It was impossible, however, to ignore the obvious success of the new technology and the Post

Office agent at Holyhead was instructed to consider the relative merits of steam and sail. He embarked on the *Talbot* from Holyhead at 8.20 a.m. on 14 April 1820 and arrived at Howth at 5 p.m., eight and a half hours later. The Post Office packet ship, the *Spencer*, which had left at 8.15 a.m. the same day did not arrive until 4.25 a.m. the following morning, a passage of twenty hours and ten minutes. This experiment put the question beyond doubt and the Post Office commissioned two new steamships for the cross channel route: the *Lightning* and the *Meteor*, their very names conveying the new and exciting sense of speed that was to be experienced by those who travelled on them. On 11 August 1821 the seal of royal approval was bestowed on the new steam service when King George IV crossed to Howth on the *Lightning*: an imprint of his rather dainty feet is still to be seen on the pier. He left Ireland, however, from Kingstown and it would be that harbour which would replace Howth as the Post Office packet station. Kingstown offered maritime advantages in terms of approach and safety but railway developments also bolstered its claims just as they would support Holyhead on the other side of the Irish Sea. Under an agreement of 6 April 1835 with the Dublin & Kingstown Railway Company, mails were conveyed from Westland Row station to and from Kingstown in specially constructed coaches and would later be brought right up to the side of the waiting mail boats.

Left: Between 1826 and 1849 mail boats sailed from Kingstown to Liverpool as well as Holyhead. In June 1849, Liverpool was abandoned as an Irish packet station. (Stephen Ferguson)

Right: The *Harlequin*, a 16 gun brig, later renamed *Sprightly*, served on the Kingstown-Holyhead route as one of the Admiralty's packets commanded by Mr. Moon R.N. (With kind permission from the National Maritime Museum, Greenwich, London)

HER MAJESTY'S STEAM PACKETS
Between DUBLIN and HOLYHEAD.

Otter, Lieut. Jones, R.N.	*Doterel*, Mr. Gray, R.N.
Zephyr, Lieut. Smail, R.N.	*Sprightly*, Mr. Moon, R.N.

Sail alternately every Morning at Nine o'clock, from KINGSTOWN, with the Mail and Government Depatches.

Agent at Holyhead, John Kains, R.N.

N.B.—A Train starts from the Railway station, Westland-row, every half-hour till 10 P.M. The Packet will lie alongside the New Quay two hours previous to that time for the reception of passengers.—Packet-Office, 17, Upper Sackville-street, Dublin.

HER MAJESTY'S STEAM PACKETS
Between DUBLIN and LIVERPOOL.

Medusa, Lieut. Philipps, R.N.	*Urgent*, Mr. Emerson, R.N.
Merlin, Lieut. Keane, R.N.	*Medina*, Mr. Smithett, R.N.

Sail alternately every Evening, at half-past 9 o'clock, from KINGSTOWN, with the Mail and Government Despatches, arriving at LIVERPOOL the next Morning in time for the Train leaving LIVERPOOL at half-past 10 at noon, enabling Passengers to reach LONDON the same evening.

Agent at Liverpool, Thomas Bevis, R.N.

N.B.—A Train starts from the Railway station, Westland-row, every half-hour till 10 P.M. The Packet will lie alongside the New Quay two hours previous to that time for the reception of passengers.—Packet-Office, 17, upper Sackville-street, Dublin.

Above Holyhead harbour stands this memorial to John Skinner RN, the popular American-born packet captain who plied the Dublin-Holyhead route from 1799 until he was swept overboard off Holyhead in 1832.
(Stephen Ferguson)

While the mail is long gone and its railway importance much diminished, Holyhead today remains a busy passenger and commercial port for traffic between Ireland and Britain.
(Stephen Ferguson)

Opposite page: A beautiful early photograph of Kingstown, c1865–70, showing an unidentified mail boat at the pier, the George IV monument and a warship anchored in the harbour.
(Frederick H. Mares/Davisonphoto)

Kingstown, Mail Packet Station, Co. Dublin.

Picture postcards were extremely popular in the early twentieth century and there are many views of a bustling Kingstown harbour. (An Post Museum & Archive)

The Holyhead to Kingstown mail contract

In 1823 the City of Dublin Steam Packet Company (CDSPC) was established. Over the next century it would overcome political pressures and competitive challenges to win an enviable reputation for the reliability, speed and technological innovation of its ships. The close relationship which it would build with the Irish Post Office, through its possession of the Holyhead to Kingstown mail contract, would play a vital part in its success with the exacting demands of Post Office time-tables necessitating a punctuality which was much appreciated by the travelling public.

The emblem of the City of Dublin Steam Packet Company is still to be seen on the site of its former premises on Eden Quay in Dublin. (Stephen Ferguson)

It was a relationship, however, which took time to develop and the Post Office was not easily persuaded that the private sector might operate ships more efficiently and more cost effectively than Government. In March 1824 the Company had sought permission to carry the mails from Liverpool to Dublin but the proposal had been dismissed. The Company was not discouraged, however, by the Government's stance and, in April 1826, submitted another memorial offering to carry the mails at times suitable to the Post Office and on any remuneration decided by the Postmaster General. Despite its advantageous offer, Government was still not ready to accept the idea of private sector involvement in mails conveyance and it was not until 1839 that the Company's patient persistence was rewarded when it was given a contract to supplement the Government packet service, managed since 1837 by the Admiralty rather than the Post Office, from Howth to Holyhead. It would provide a day mail service from Kingstown to Liverpool at a cost of £9,000 p.a. The Company undertook to leave Kingstown daily between 4 p.m. and 7 p.m. and Liverpool between 5 p.m. and 8 p.m. and agreed to have eight vessels on hand if required and accept a £300 penalty for each service failure.

The CDSPC won its first Post Office contract at a significant time. The packet boat service was satisfactorily managed by the Admiralty but operating costs were substantial. What altered the position was the influence of two major social developments which had a marked impact on communication, both physical and postal, between Britain and Ireland. One was pressure for Post Office reform, especially in relation to postage rates, which were very high. This, largely through the zeal of Rowland Hill, culminated in the introduction of uniform penny post throughout the United Kingdom which, in turn, generated an increase in postal volumes. The other was widespread railway development, firstly with lines from London to Manchester, Birmingham and Liverpool and subsequently to Chester and Holyhead. The construction of these railway lines brought great improvements in the speed of travel and affected decisions on whether Liverpool, Holyhead or other Welsh harbours would become the principal port through which mail and passengers would be brought to Dublin. It was a time when a great deal of money hung on the investment decisions of both Government and railwaymen and the Post Office mail contract was an important factor in the deliberations of several shrewd Victorian businessmen and engineers. In the end, Holyhead won out over its rivals and the CDSPC, which had been efficiently providing the mail service on the Liverpool route, believed it was well placed to tender for the Holyhead to Kingstown mail contract. This arose when the Government, on foot of a parliamentary investigation into the operation of the Kingstown to Holyhead mail services in April 1849, found that the City of Dublin's ships were cheaper to run than the Government's Admiralty packets.

Tenders, consequently, were sought in December 1849. Competition for the Holyhead to Kingstown mail contract was expected from the Chester and Holyhead Railway Company which, in conjunction with its ally, the powerful London & North Western Railway Company (LNWR), ran the Irish Mail train to Euston station in London. In the event, only the CDSPC tendered in line with the terms of the competition but the railway companies were able, as they would be on a number of subsequent occasions, to exert influence behind the scenes so that the CDSPC was obliged to reduce its original offer. The Chester & Holyhead company felt it had done enough to make the contract uneconomic for the CDSPC but was outmanoeuvred by the Dublin company which, in its longer-term strategic interest, submitted a very low tender of £25,000 on 5 March 1850. It was a bold move on the

This page of the CDSPC's journal for the week beginning 14 October 1844 records mail as the cargo for several of its ships. (Courtesy of the National Library of Ireland)

part of the CDSPC's Managing Director, William Watson, but it proved to be the right one and for the next seventy years, punctuated by regular tussles with its rival, the LNWR, the City of Dublin Steam Packet Company would hold on to the Holyhead & Kingstown (H&K) mail contract.[8] Watson's sons, another William (knighted in 1897) and Edward would successfully guide the Company into the twentieth century and in the end it would succumb not so much to the commercial might of the great railway company as to the incalculable follies of war and the changed realities of Irish politics.

The new CDSPC service began on 1 June 1850. The Company had purchased two of the ships, the *Llewellyn* and the *St. Columba,* which had plied the route under the Admiralty and to these it added the *Eblana,* and a brand new ship, the *Prince Arthur,* which started

operation in June 1851. At that time the normal passage between Holyhead and Kingstown was four hours and forty minutes with an average speed of twelve knots but weather could affect speeds significantly with the occasional sub-four hour passage to be set against others that were close to seven hours. The tender which the Company had won had made no stipulations concerning passenger accommodation and while the Post Office was quite happy with the service, there were complaints from passengers. Concern for female passengers, in particular, was notable with ladies 'frequently being obliged to lie on the floor in such numbers as to render it impossible to move about the over-crowded cabins'.[9] Over the following decade, various discussions on potential improvements to the Dublin-London service took place between the Post Office and the three contracting companies, the CDSPC, the LNWR and the Chester & Holyhead

Manoeuvring a large ship within Kingstown harbour and in close proximity to many smaller craft called for seamanship of a high order. (W.D. Hemphill MD/Davisonphoto)

railway. The latter had increasingly come under the control of the LNWR which, besides its British railway business, also operated its own ships on the Irish Sea route. This, especially on the question of "through bookings", caused tension with the CDSPC. Keen to provide first class ships, the CDSPC undertook to build four new ships to service the mail contract. These replaced their existing vessels and were named after the four Irish provinces, Ulster, Munster, Leinster and Connaught. In Kingstown, a new jetty, the Carlisle pier, was completed just before Christmas 1859 while improvements were also made to the Admiralty pier in Holyhead. The construction of the Carlisle pier at Kingstown meant that trains could draw up alongside the ship, saving time on mail and passenger transfers. One other development of that time, which would subsequently add to the importance of the Irish Sea

service, was the offer by the Cunard company to call in to Queenstown (Cobh) on transatlantic voyages to take on and land mails at that port. Though less than enthusiastic, the Postmaster General agreed to accept this offer on a trial basis. His decision made it possible for transatlantic mails to be advantageously routed through Ireland leading to an increase in volumes sorted on board the Irish mail boats and mail trains. During the American Civil War's *Trent* affair the importance of that postal route came to prominence when, early on January 7th 1862, the *Ulster,* carrying an urgent dispatch from British diplomats in America, played its part in averting war between the United Kingdom and the United States.

In his report for 1860, the Postmaster General, Lord Stanley of Alderley, reported on the success of what was termed the 'new Irish Postal Service', the cornerstone of which was the achievement of an eleven-and-a-half-hour journey time between London and Dublin, a maximum gain of over three hours and ten minutes on the old service. The benefit to the Post Office was actually greater than the mere reduction in travelling time because it gained also from the efficiencies to be made through sorting letters on the ships and on the railway's Travelling Post Office (TPO) carriages. The PMG had regretfully to confess, however, that 'the penalties for delay, on which the Department greatly relied for ensuring punctuality, are temporarily suspended, owing to the state of the present pier accommodation at Holyhead'.[10] This was a reference to the Government's failure to improve pier accommodation in accordance with clause 11 of the mail contract. The timber jetty at Holyhead, for example, was not only inadequate but unsafe, the captain of the *Connaught* noting that, on 2 November 1861, he had five hawsers carried away while trying to come alongside. 'I feared', he said, that 'the ship would get adrift altogether: had she done so nothing could have saved her from going on the rocks'.[11] The ultimate benefit conferred on the letter-writing public under the new contract was that mails which left Dublin or London in the morning would, in normal circumstances, be assured of making the final evening delivery in each city or connecting with an onward dispatch for provincial and continental destinations.

The contract which had come into force on 1 October 1860 expired in 1874 but nothing was done about this until June 1882 when new tenders for the sea and land elements of the journey were sought and received. The CDSPC offered to provide the sea service at £60,000 with the Provinces while the LNWR tendered at £66,000 for their four vessels, (the Kingdoms – *Hibernia, Anglia, Scotia and Cambria*), which operated from Dublin's North Wall. The LNWR, however, also offered a combined sea and rail tender of £76,000 between London and the North Wall. This combined offer, which exploited the LNWR's strength in both sea and rail, was attractive to the Government and duly accepted by the Treasury in January 1883. The consequence was uproar in Ireland, with debates in Westminster and with Irish Peers and MPs, business representatives and even the Provost and Fellows of Trinity College calling on Gladstone, then First Lord of the Treasury, to right the great wrong that had been done to Ireland. As discussion continued and investigations, led by Edward Gray, MP for County Carlow, revealed close

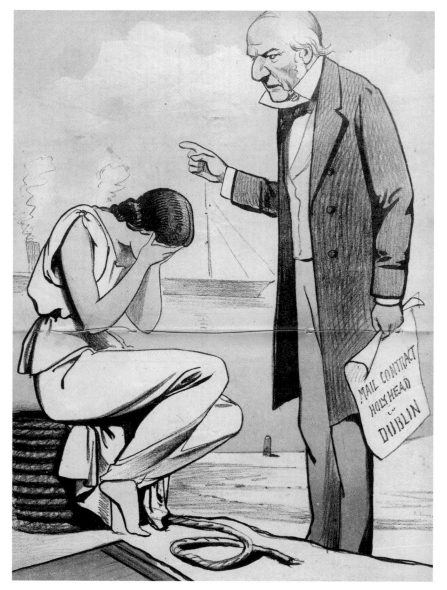

A contemporary political cartoon, under the heading 'Go, Deceiver, Go', shows Ireland weeping as Gladstone explains that the CDSPC has lost the mail contract to the LNWR's apparently better offer. (An Post Museum & Archive)

links between certain Westminster politicians and the directors of the LNWR, it began to seem that the CDSPC was being unfairly squeezed out of the Irish Sea mail contract in favour of British interests as represented by the LNWR. Subsequent revelations confirmed that the savings apparently on offer from the LNWR's tender had not been correctly calculated. Indignation at the conduct of the Government was widespread and with Irish MPs of all political colours united – Liberals, Conservatives and Home Rulers – the LNWR contract was not confirmed by Parliament, and the Postmaster General was asked on 18 April 1883 to seek new tenders for the separate sea and land sections of the journey. On this occasion the Postmaster General accepted the City of Dublin's offer of £84,000 p.a. The contract time for the journey was set at 4 hours and 7 minutes (4 hours and two minutes on the inward leg) including mails transfer times. The Company's existing ships, fitted with more efficient boilers, and a new reserve vessel, the *Ireland*, were to provide the service and the contract price would include the cost of conveying parcels – a new service just introduced by the Post Office – as well as letters.

In 1895 the contract came up for renewal again and in July the Post Office invited tenders for the H&K route. Those interested were given the particulars of the existing service with details of the vessels employed and the mails transfer times on each leg of the journey. They were then asked to submit tenders setting out the terms on which they would provide services that would match the existing sea journey time or improve it by either half an hour or a whole hour. The Postmaster General's notice stated that he had already written to the LNWR inviting it to make an offer not only for the rail portion of the journey from London to Holyhead – on which of course it was the only operator – but also for the entire route from London to Kingstown. This direct approach to the LNWR was seen in Ireland as unfair to local firms, essentially the CDSPC, which submitted various tenders putting forward options for maintaining the existing service and cutting the journey by thirty and sixty minutes respectively. The shorter journey time came at the cost of an increased subsidy and faster ships but the Company's directors, no doubt hoping that a quarter century's satisfactory service would count for something, were optimistic. When they heard that not one of their tenders had found favour with the Post Office and that the PMG found their terms exorbitant, they were worried. The Company Secretary wrote to Spencer Walpole, the Post Office Secretary in London, urgently seeking a meeting with Arnold Morley, the PMG, and explaining that his directors were most anxious that no action on their part might interfere with the public demand for the improvement and acceleration of the service. Irish chambers of commerce were quick to make representations to the Post Office, regretting its 'customary want of enterprise' and insisting it end the dead-lock on the question and obey 'the universal law of progress which is the distinctive feature of the present time.' [12]

It was the Company's acute appreciation of public demand that had, ironically, worked against it in the tender process because the Post Office, influenced by the Treasury on financial matters and by the Admiralty on nautical matters, was actually less interested in a more efficient and faster service and more interested in

A study in steam: transferring the mail took only a few minutes and, with contractual penalties for every minute's delay, it was the practice of the mail boat captains to await the mails with steam up. (William Cavanagh/ Davisonphoto)

economy. For several years, the Treasury had pointed to the high cost of the Holyhead and Kingstown packet service which absorbed the greater part of the domestic packet service budget. In 1875, for instance, the H&K subsidy was £85,900. This compared with just £9,000 for the British Post Office portion of the Dover to Calais route, £105,000 for the Liverpool to New York/Boston route and just £65,000 for the entire Africa correspondence. The Admiralty, for its part, had provided advice that was based on mail boats that lacked the capacity to deliver an accelerated service. It is worth noting too that the goal of improving facilities for passenger traffic between the two countries was no longer as important to the Government as it had once been, given that there were now a number of companies

providing such services on the Irish Sea. When, consequently, the CDSPC put in tenders that envisaged the construction of four new ships, larger and faster than the existing vessels with better accommodation for both passengers and mails, it had to overcome a degree of resistance on the part of Post Office management. The Company's representatives argued that ships of increased power with additional space were essential to provide a regular service of the speed and quality desired and that some margin must be allowed both in terms of engine capacity and mails volume growth. The PMG insisted the Post Office had not sought increased mail or passenger accommodation nor had he, moreover, had any complaint that the present boats were deficient in either respect.

There was a certain amount of disingenuousness on both sides. The Post Office hoped to get an improved service at no extra cost and was happy to play down the increase in mail volumes and the need for more space. For its part, the CDSPC wanted to benefit from first-class new ships that could offer passengers speed and facilities that would be superior to anything that its rivals in the LNWR could provide. Conscious that maintaining their hold on the mail contract was essential to their business, the CDSPC wrote to the PMG on St. Stephen's Day 1894 offering to provide the service at the reduced fee of £125,000 p.a. (the same sum it had sought back in 1883) if the Post Office would extend the contract from 20 to 25 years and also move the London and Dublin day departure times back by at least half an hour. There matters rested for some time as the Post Office and the Treasury weighed up the options. Deadlock on the matter, indeed, was

R.M.S. *Munster*

An attractive *Munster* card by James Walker & Co., colour printers, of Dame Street and Rathmines. The design was one common to all four Provinces. (An Post Museum & Archive)

The new and accelerated Irish mail service came into effect on 1 April 1897 and in his annual report the Postmaster General, the Duke of Norfolk, conceded that the new packet ships provided 'greatly improved accommodation for Mails and passengers' and had 'in every way proved satisfactory.'[14] The contracted journey time (including time to transfer the mails) was 3 hours and 37 minutes on the outward voyage from Holyhead and, at 3 hours and 32 minutes, a little shorter on the inward passage from Kingstown. In practice, the CDSPC expected to perform the crossing in an average of 2 hours and 45 minutes. A penalty clause meant that every minute's delay would cost the CDSPC £1-14s. and £100 for any occasion on which the vessel was not ready to sail. The new timetable is given at Table 1 overleaf.

The *Irish Times* of 31 March enthusiastically welcomed the new ships, anticipating a 'new era in… Channel travel' and applauding the new postal arrangements which allowed Dublin businesses more time to deal with their daily correspondence from Britain. The same day's *Freeman's Journal*, however, had harsh words for the GPO since the arrangements envisaged for accelerating provincial mails had not been put in place, local managers, it claimed, having been preoccupied instead with 'the demon of parsimonious economy'. The editor warned those responsible in Dublin's GPO to consider 'whether it is, in the end, more serviceable to themselves to court adverse public criticism or to cater for the public convenience.' In fairness to my colleagues of yesterday, the Postmaster General had postponed final arrangements in deference to the House of Commons and in his report thought it 'a matter for congratulation that it has been found possible to

the impression made on the mind of one prominent Dublin businessman, William Martin Murphy, who had wide-ranging interests in the transport sector. On 18 March 1895, he wrote to the PMG to observe that since the CDSPC did not seem to have been awarded the mail contract he would be prepared to make a tender himself, his 'project contemplating an Irish company and the building of the ships in Ireland'. [13] Behind the scenes discussions were, however, taking place and the Irish Chief Secretary, the Liberal John Morley, and Irish MPs were doing their best to exert pressure on behalf of the CDSPC, arguing for the needs of Ireland as a whole for an improved mail and passenger service. In the end, the contract was awarded to the Company on the basis of a 20-year term running until 31 March 1917, a subsidy of £100,000 and a sea passage accelerated by half an hour.

An interesting photograph showing two ships berthed stern to stern at the Carlisle pier in 1909: the black-funnelled ship is the mail boat while the other is an LNWR vessel. Berthing rights led to acrimonious disputes between the two companies. (Davisonphoto/ Chapman Livingston Collection)

Table 1 H&K Packet accelerated mails schedule 1897

	NIGHT MAIL		DAY MAIL	
	Old times	New times	Old times	New times
Down journey				
London Euston – dep.	8.20pm	8.45pm	7.15am	7.15am
Holyhead – train arrives	2.35am	2.25am	1.28pm	1.28pm
Kingstown – train leaves	6.42am	6.00am	5.35pm	5.05pm
Dublin – arr.	6.54am	6.14am	5.47pm	5.17pm
Up journey				
Dublin – dep.	7.35pm	8.25pm	7.05am	7.35am
Kingstown – arr.	7.50pm	8.40pm	7.20am	7.50am
Holyhead Pier – dep.	11.52pm	12.12am	11.22am	11.22am
London Euston – arr.	6.15am	6.10am	5.45pm	5.45pm

and to have a definite naval escort arrangement put in place. In the end, the Post Office declined to assume the war risk, said a replacement for the *Connaught* would be considered when private ship building was again allowed and referred the escort question to the Admiralty. On 5 August 1918 agreement was reached for another temporary renewal on the basis of a £78,000 subsidy, the Company to take on the war risk. In 1920, the contract would be lost to the LNWR.

shorten the night journeys by about an hour and the day journeys by about half an hour each way.'[15] The speed of the Holyhead to Kingstown passage, compared with the seven and a half hour crossing which had been usual sixty years earlier when Queen Victoria had come to the throne, was certainly a remarkable improvement.

The renewal of the H&K mail contract arose in 1917 but, owing to the war, only temporary continuation arrangements were put in place. A subsidy of £78,000 was agreed between the Post Office and the CDSPC and when the matter came up again in 1918 the Post Office offered only a reduced figure of £60,000. The Company was prepared to consider this on the understanding that the Post Office would assume the war insurance risk. It was also pressing to have a new ship built at Laird's to replace the *Connaught*, sunk in the English Channel,

Richard Beechey's 1868 painting of the
Leinster as she approaches the entrance
to Kingstown harbour is a study in graceful
tranquillity. (Private collection)

THE "ULSTER" PADDLE-STEAMER RECENTLY LAUNCHED AT BIRKENHEAD, BELONGING TO THE CITY OF DUBLIN STEAM-PACKET COMPANY.

The *Leinster* and her sisters

Few would have imagined in October 1860 when the CDSPC's four new ships started work for the Post Office that their names were destined, in the mind of the Irish public, to become synonymous with the Kingstown to Holyhead crossing. The idea of using the names of the four Irish provinces, *Ulster, Munster, Leinster* and *Connaught* may owe its inspiration to the Chester & Holyhead Railway which in 1848, at the time it expected to win the H&K mail contract, had named its paddle-steamers after the four kingdoms of the British Isles, *Hibernia, Anglia, Scotia* and *Cambria.*

While all four ships, both in their 1860 and 1896 incarnations, were virtually identical, the *Leinster* was the one which gradually assumed a slight precedence over her sisters. She had, it is true, been the first of the new CDSPC ships to be completed and the Post Office agreed that she might begin operating in August 1860, a little ahead of the formal contract date, but she was not the fastest: that distinction belonged to the *Connaught,* which on its measured mile test run, became the first steamer in the world to exceed 18 knots. She was built in London, at the Samuda yard, while the three other Provinces were built by Laird Brothers of Birkenhead.

They were all paddle steamers, vessels of 2000 tons each with engines in proportion, and in dimension measured 334 feet long, 35 feet beam and 21 feet in depth. The hull and funnels were painted black with the inside, upper works, paddle boxes and boats finished in white paint. With four funnels, they were remarkably striking vessels and, in technical specification, far ahead of their contemporaries. Their looks and their performance combined to make an impression and the general fit-out and standard was high. There was spacious first-class accommodation, deck cabins were provided amidships and sleeping cabins for first and second class passengers were located forward, thus addressing to a great extent the complaints voiced earlier by passengers. From the point of view of the Post Office, the big innovation was the provision, under clause eight of the new mail contract, of a sorting office on board so that mails could be sorted and prepared for onward delivery while the ships were at sea.

The new ships were faster than those they replaced, generally managing a speed of 14.5 knots, a three-knot increase over their predecessors, on the sixty-four mile journey between Kingstown and Holyhead. Fitted with

Opposite page: This engraving of the *Ulster* shows that nautical wisdom in 1860 was not yet ready completely to abandon canvas in favour of steam. (Courtesy of Wirral Archives Service)

oscillating engines of 750nhp, they were not only faster but also more powerful ships and so the difference between fair and foul weather passages was reduced. There were still difficult days of course. One such was 9 February 1861 when the *Leinster* left Kingstown as usual but, facing a hard east-north-east hurricane which stove in her turtle-back deck and the sorting office skylight, was forced to return to harbour. The weather on that occasion was so bad that Captain Boyd of the *Ajax* guardship lost his life in an attempt to rescue the crew of a ship that had been driven onto the east pier. An obelisk on that pier stands today as a monument to his bravery.

The Provinces maintained wonderful regularity over the years in their time-keeping. The Post Office penalty clause was a financial incentive, of course, but there was also a great sense of pride in the Company and its crew. Storms had to be overcome but fog sometimes posed a greater danger to the ships. On one occasion, in very dense fog, the *Connaught* on its way to Holyhead collided with the LNWR's *Cambria* coming from the opposite direction. One of the *Cambria's* paddle-boxes smashed into and under the port paddle-box of the *Connaught*. The two ships were locked fast for eight hours in a calm sea until the crew could cut their way out and allow both ships to proceed slowly to Holyhead. Some years later, in 1902, the *Leinster* ran into the Kish lightship, the *Albatross*, again in dense fog, and sank it. Through the quick thinking of Captain Birch, who would lose his life not far from that spot in 1918, the lightship's crew was rescued and little damage done to the mail boat.

The *Connaught* about to enter Holyhead harbour in May 1885. She was the first ship, during her trials, known to have steamed at over eighteen knots. (Gwynedd Archives Service)

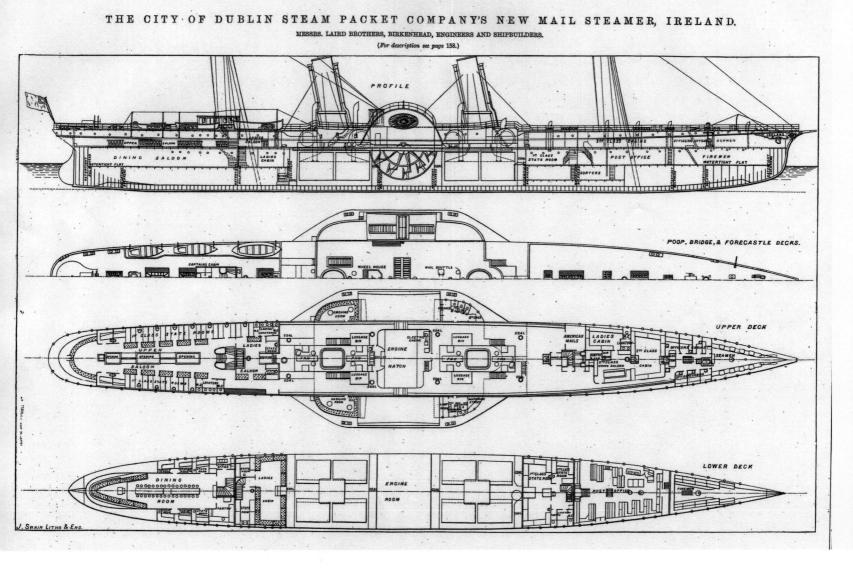

THE CITY OF DUBLIN STEAM PACKET COMPANY'S NEW MAIL STEAMER, IRELAND.

MESSRS. LAIRD BROTHERS, BIRKENHEAD, ENGINEERS AND SHIPBUILDERS.

(*For description see page 158.*)

The *Ireland*, built by Laird Brothers for the CDSPC, joined the Provinces as a mail boat in 1885. She was larger and faster than them and in terms of postal facilities served as a template for the Mark II ships in 1896. (Courtesy of Wirral Archives Service)

The vessels underwent a substantial re-fit in 1885-86. Work on the boilers, during which the four funnels were reduced to two, increased their speed, a rather remarkable outcome for ships which were 25 years old, and enabled them to continue in service until 1896-97. They had been joined in 1885 on the H&K mail run by a new paddle steamer, the *Ireland*, which was about 20 per cent greater in tonnage than the existing ships. She made her trial, against a stiff breeze, on 26 August that year sailing from Kingstown's east pier to the Holyhead breakwater in three hours and eight minutes. The Post Office's nautical advisor was so satisfied with this speed that he did not bother to take the return leg when the ship made a record-breaking passage of two hours and forty-six minutes, proving she could maintain an average speed of over twenty knots and making her the fastest passenger steamer afloat, a matter of considerable pride not only to the Company and its employees but to the nation as a whole which felt vindicated in the award of the Post Office contract to an Irish firm.

By 1895, when the CDSPC had managed to negotiate the renewal of the mail contract with the Post Office, the Provinces definitely needed to be replaced. The contract was executed on 1 July 1895 and the CDSPC immediately placed an order with Laird's of Birkenhead for the construction of four new Provinces, each of 3,000 gross tonnage. The *Ulster* was the first of the ships to be completed in June 1896 and a distinguished gathering of local and Dublin dignitaries cheered the Duchess of Abercorn as she named the ship.

William Watson, managing director of the CDSPC, proposed the toast of 'Laird Brothers, Birkenhead' remarking that the firm had 'always done exactly

Opposite page: One of the CDSPC's mail boats leaving Kingstown, its funnels belching smoke. The four funnel configuration for these paddle steamers was reduced to two during a refit in 1886. (Courtesy of the National Library of Ireland)

what they undertook to do'. Replying, William Laird was pleased to say that the connection between the CDSPC and his firm was a long one and 'since the first transaction in 1833 his firm had built 17 vessels for the City of Dublin Company. (Hear, hear.)'

The *Leinster*, though generally represented as ship 613, is actually 612, as shown on the signed contract document and by the launch dates. The *Munster* is 613 and the numbers were accidentally misplaced on the official list. The four new ships were every bit as revolutionary as their 1860 predecessors. Twin-screw rather than paddle ships and powered by triple-expansion 9,000 horse power engines, they were the first Irish Sea steamers to exceed 24 knots, making them amongst the fastest passenger vessels in the world. Their improved eight-cylinder engines were about three times more powerful than the previous ones and, with the scheduled time allowing two hours and forty-five minutes for the passage, the ships could comfortably achieve the half hour saving required for the new accelerated Irish mail service. On its port to port speed trial, the *Leinster* covered the passage in just two hours and twenty-three minutes, a remarkable time which would not be surpassed until the introduction of Stena's HSS ferries in recent times.

Flush-decked, the nautical eye would have observed that everything in the lines of the hull, the rake of the masts and funnels and construction of deck accommodation indicated that the *Leinster* and her sisters were built for speed. Nothing, however, had been sacrificed in the way of first and second-class passenger accommodation with comforts and modern facilities that were on a par with some of the best hotels. The cabins, dining rooms,

drawing and smoking rooms were spacious and well-appointed and there was electric lighting provided throughout the ship. 'Hot and cold, plunge, and shower baths' were available so that, as one reviewer put it 'the voyager, wearied by a long railway ride, has every aid to recruit his energies while in transit across the Irish Sea.' His only criticism was that the speed of the vessels limited the time for 'the enjoyment of such pleasant surroundings to the shortest possible limits'!

Irish pride in the City of Dublin's ships was strong and increased on those occasions when one of them was used to bring royal visitors to the country, as when the Prince of Wales accepted the offer of a special steamer and travelled on the *Ulster* in 1905. Addressing shareholders at the 184th half yearly meeting at the Company's offices in Eden Quay on 10 May 1910, Sir William Watson, the managing director, having voiced the meeting's sorrow

on the death of Edward VII and declared a 3% dividend, allowed himself a few words to express what was, no doubt, the general feeling of the proprietors:

> *The Company has been the sea contractor for his Majesty's Mails between Kingstown and Holyhead for a period of sixty years; the Company is the oldest steam packet company in existence, and we trust the support we have had in the past will be continued for the future, and the Company retain the position of sea carriers of the Mails at least until steamers are superseded by air ships or a tunnel made underneath St. George's Channel.*

Over the years, there developed friendships between regular passengers and members of the crew and stories of particular characters became the stuff of conversation. One such was Richard Simon Triphook who had been born in Castletownsend in county Cork,

A fine view of the *Leinster* with St Michael's church, all but the steeple destroyed by fire in 1965, towering over its funnels in the background. (Neville Cook)

Published shortly after its launch in 1896, these are rare photographs of the *Leinster's* interior decoration. They give an idea of the comfortable facilities provided for passengers on the CDSPC's mail boats. Shown here are The Ladies' Saloon, The Smoke Room and The Dining Saloon. (© Royal Mail Group Ltd, Courtesy of The Postal Museum)

Right: Captain John Thomas of the *Leinster* adopts a more traditional pose for his portrait. (An Post Museum & Archive)

Above & top left: Cork-born Richard Triphook, 'Old Trip', was one of the CDSPC's most famous characters captaining the *Ulster* in its paddle-steamer incarnations. Pictured here with his hat at a jaunty angle and his faithful dog Chance on his lap, he was sufficiently famous to have a piece of popular music dedicated to him. (Courtesy of the Board of Trinity College Dublin, the University of Dublin) Music - (An Post Museum & Archive)

became a commander in the Royal Navy and retired as captain of the *Ulster* on the Kingstown-Holyhead run. Respected and much loved by crew and passengers, "Old Trip" was not beyond giving people a fright in the interest of his ship's efficiency. On one occasion, when he had set the crew to a fire drill, he quietly jumped off the paddle box into the sea, shouting as he fell, and when they had got him on board again, he looked at his watch, said 'Not bad: 4 minutes' and calmly went below to change his clothes. Wherever he went he was accompanied by his devoted fox terrier, Chance, which on the occasion of this unscheduled emergency rescue drill, jumped overboard after his master, also to be safely rescued!

Of the four Provinces, the *Leinster* was perhaps the public's favourite. Not only was it fast and comfortable but its captain and crew had a particular reputation as entertaining companions and it had, over the years, acquired a certain *cachet* which gave it a slight social edge over its sister ships. The *Irish Times*' "Fashionable Intelligence" column, for example, reported regularly on the celebrities who would be travelling on it. Irish MPs going to Westminster were fond of the ship – they got free passage from the Company as a mark of thanks for their influential parliamentary support – and it was patronised too by many wealthy, titled and landed people. You never knew whom you might meet even in the midst of war – just a couple of days before it was torpedoed, the king of Portugal, Manuel II, was on board – and the *Leinster* became, in a sense, the place to be seen and the ideal venue for catching up on all the news and gossip.

The message on this CDSPC card of 1909 to Mrs. Beringer in Wolverhampton contains the recipe for a pleasant sea journey, 'had good lunch then to sleep', and the most reassuring phrase of all 'not s--k'! (An Post Museum & Archive)

Sorting the mail

Mail on the mail boats would have been sorted in the traditional way, inserted into canvas bags and labelled with the correct destination labels. (Stephen Ferguson)

suggest to establish a more Speedy and Commodious Communications between the two Capitals'.

The fifteen members appointed to the committee were asked to examine not only the expeditious conveyance of mails but also to consider the transport of troops, the convenience of the public and the particular needs of Irish members of parliament in attending Westminster. It is a wide-ranging and interesting report with much useful information on ships, harbours, mails and passenger traffic and the commercial rivalry between the companies engaged on the London to Dublin route.

What is of particular note is the discussion that takes place on the value of providing post office sorting facilities on the ships. In its quest to improve the efficiency of the postal service between Dublin and London, the Select Committee was keen to examine what effect on-board sorting would have in improving delivery times in Dublin and the rest of Ireland. Consideration of ship sorting naturally led on to discussion of the use of Travelling Post Offices on Irish railways. At this time, while there were some TPOs employed in England, there were none used in Ireland.

The CDSPC's 1896-97 mail boats were equipped with good post office facilities but the idea of providing sorting offices on board had its origin many years before that. In May 1853 a select committee of the House of Commons had been appointed to investigate and report upon the communication channel between London and Dublin in an effort, as the terms of reference put it, to discover 'what Improvements modern Science can

The advantages to be had from the use of both marine and railway sorting offices tended to be clearer to members of the committee and some external witnesses than it was to the officials of the Post Office who, not for the first time, come across as rather conservative in their outlook.

Discussion of the topic first emerges in the evidence offered by Cusack P. Roney, an Irishman who had a successful career in railways and ended up as Secretary of the Eastern Counties Railway. Replying to a question from the committee Chairman, Henry Herbert of Muckross House and MP for Kerry, Roney said he believed that

> *A large saving of time would be effected in the disposal of the letters when they arrive at Kingstown…*
> *if arrangements were made on board the boats for sorting the letters, similar to that which we all know is adopted on all the leading railways in England…*
> *I cannot see myself any reason why that could not be done in the mail rooms of mail boats, just as well as it is done in the Post-office vans on the railways;*[16]

He saw no practical difficulties in fitting up a suitable mail room on the ships and envisaged the Post Office assigning to this task 'a regular staff of clerks, who should sort the letters for the different streets of Dublin in the journey down from London to Dublin and *vice versa*' with the post then being passed on to the railway TPOs which he felt must soon be introduced in Ireland. While Roney had a very clear picture of what the future held, he admitted that while he was unaware of its nature, it was 'just possible that there may be a Post-office objection' to the plan. The Post Office objection

to the introduction of a packet sorting office was stated simply by G. C. Cornwall, Secretary of the Irish Post Office. When asked by Herbert what his objection to the idea was, he replied 'I do not think it would accelerate the matter'. While Cornwall was pleased to have the mail boat arrive earlier in Kingstown, he saw the time gained as an opportunity to move to a slightly earlier dispatch of all mail from the GPO in Dublin. The incoming English mail was just part of a much larger volume of post that came in to the GPO between 5 and 6 a.m. each morning from the whole of Ireland and which had to be sorted and dispatched within a very tight time-frame. His boss, Colonel Maberly, who was Secretary of the Post Office in London, saw little advantage at all in sorting mail on the ships. In his view, it would have to be re-sorted in Dublin 'because you could not trust to the sorting' since it would be quite unreasonable to expect two or three clerks on the ship to know the entirety of the Irish sorting circulation system. When pressed by members of the committee, he said Ireland had five or six hundred post towns and another 1500 post offices so when, for example, letters came addressed to

> *"Sir Robert Ferguson, the Farm." Who is to know where "the Farm" is? But the man who knows the Londonderry line would know Sir Robert Ferguson's address, and would correct the misdirection.*[17]

The Committee, in response, then suggested that mail bags might simply be made up on the ship for major Irish destinations like Cork and Belfast but Maberly was not to be easily soothed in his objections and he replied that sorting to the larger Irish cities was already undertaken in London so while a little time might be

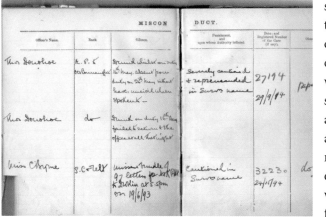

saved through the introduction of a mail room on the ships 'it would be very small, not above a quarter of an hour or 20 minutes'. Maberly, of course, was well known for scepticism towards certain aspects of Post Office reform and a reluctance to embrace what he saw as unnecessary change but there were certainly practical limits to what could be done in terms of general Post Office operations. There was no point, for instance, collecting or delivering letters when people were in bed. Cornwall, the Dublin GPO boss, summed it up well when he said that

> *the most satisfactory communication to the public, between any two distant points, is that which affords as late a dispatch as possible in the evening from the one end, and as early an arrival as possible in the morning at the other end.*[18]

While the Post Office attitude to the initial ideas for sorting letters on the mail boats was not encouraging, the basic principle was established by the discussion at this Select Committee and when it was put to Maberly that if larger ships with proper staff and facilities for sorting were engaged on the Holyhead to Kingstown route, it would surely lessen the labour of sorting in the Dublin GPO, he had to concede the point:

> *Of course, if you could sort the letters coming from England, so that you had only to carry the bags in to the Dublin Post-office, it would be an advantage.*

When, consequently, the first "Provinces" were put on the route in 1860, they came duly fitted with sorting offices. The space was tight but the work of the Select Committee had borne fruit and the idea that mail might profitably be sorted on the sea portion as well as the land portion of its journey had been, albeit reluctantly, accepted by the Post Office. A Travelling Post Office on the Chester to Holyhead railway began the work of sorting the English mail for Ireland and this was continued within the mail boat's post office with the object of having Dublin and "forward" mail – that for other destinations in Ireland – prepared as far as possible for delivery or onward dispatch.

As the importance of the Post Office increased and mail volumes grew during the later Victorian years so did the amount of mail carried on the ships between Britain and Ireland. The volumes crossing from London to Dublin were heavier than those on the "up" passages and that imbalance in international traffic between the two islands persists to this day. Parcel traffic added to the significant volumes handled by staff in the post offices on board the packet ships. The greater part of parcel business was incoming English traffic and most of this was carried on the day sailings of the mail boats. Parcels leaving Ireland were generally dispatched once a week only during the 1890s. The following table sets out the marked growth in traffic between 1864, a few years after the first *Leinster* and its sister ships were introduced, and 1893, a few years before the Mark II Provinces entered service.

Table 2: Mail volumes carried on the H&K ships 1864-1893

	1864	**1873**	**1883**	**1893**
Irish mails	53,111	74,208	102,338	156,250
Foreign mails	4,172	19,153	64,878	91,003
Total mail bags	*57,283*	*93,361*	*167,216*	*247,253*
Parcel post baskets	Nil	Nil	336	26,642

An early postmark used on the H&K packet. The code letter A above the date was only used on night sailings. (An Post Museum & Archive)

While the Irish Sea mail contract was a subject which could arouse passionate interest in Ireland and periodically spark controversy both within the House of Commons and at the highest levels of Government, the day-to-day management of the mails, their conveyance and sorting, was something that was handled by the GPO in Dublin. The staff who worked on the mail boats were drawn from the men who belonged to the Dublin Sorting Office and this, until the destruction of the GPO in 1916, was based on the ground floor of the Post Office in what was then called Sackville Street and is now O'Connell Street.[19] The H&K Packet Post Office was regarded as a floating branch of Dublin's GPO. In the early years of the service, both clerks and sorters were employed in the ships' sorting offices: the clerks received an extra 5 shillings per trip and the sorters an additional 3 shillings each. By the time of the *Leinster* disaster in 1918, staff were drawn from the ranks of a grade called Sorting Clerk & Telegraphist or SC&T for short. The title reflected their training in both sides of Post Office business at the time, mail-sorting and telegraph work. Those selected for the work had to be especially good sorters with an excellent knowledge of the "circulation" or routing system for mails within the whole of the United Kingdom. Bags, of course, could not be made up for every destination but the men had to have sufficient knowledge of the entire network to know the offices and railway connections which would enable a letter to be forwarded on its way to the right destination. Working under pressure in cramped conditions, this was not a job for most men. It was disruptive to family life and called for a particularly disciplined temperament in addition to fast and accurate sorting. Mail communication was vital and the service never stopped, even at Christmas. Under the heading, Christmas Day 1889, the Post Office Circular informs staff that

> *The Day Mail from London to Dublin will be dispatched as usual, and any bags for Ireland or the Holyhead and Kingstown Packet, usually made up for this Mail at Provincial Towns on Sundays, should be made up on Christmas Day.*

There was extra pay – a trip allowance – on offer for the work, an acknowledgment by the Post Office of the pressure and inconvenience involved in the H&K Packet Post Office, and this of course was an incentive for some staff. For others, there was perhaps a more

reasonably close to the building itself and the majority of the H&K staff lived in the north inner city. Proximity to the mail boat was not necessary since it was easy to get out to Kingstown quickly on the train. The railway staff knew the Post Office men well and on the morning of 10 October 1918, one sorter, racing for the train at Westland Row, just hopped off his bicycle and shouted to a railway worker he knew to look after it till he came back.

The preliminary sorting for the mails to Britain and further afield was carried out in the GPO's sorting office. Everything, of course, was done by hand with letters sorted into the type of pigeon-hole wooden sorting frames that remained in use in many Irish post offices until very recently. The bags that were destined for the H&K packet were taken by horse and cart to Westland Row station, loaded onto the waiting mail carriage and carried on the train as far as Kingstown. The fact that the train could take the specially built spur and draw up right beside the mail boat meant that transfer of the mails to the ship was the work of just a few minutes and the ship, with steam up, could depart almost immediately for the 64-mile sea passage to Holyhead. As soon as the mailbags were on board they were opened and the letters "faced" and roughly ordered on sloping tables before being sorted into the correct circulation divisions for onward dispatch. Unloading at Holyhead and transfer of the

A formal photograph of the Dublin Post Office men who worked on the mail boats. Taken in 1910 some of these men would lose their lives on the *Leinster*. The H&K circulation book, which was the sorting Bible for railway connections, would have been familiar to all of them. (An Post Museum & Archive)

subtle attraction – the distinction and pride that came with being known as an H&K man.

The H&K Packet Post Office staff was, at the time of the *Leinster* tragedy, made up of 46 men, 3 Assistant Superintendents (Class II) and 43 SC&Ts. These men manned the mail boat post offices on the twice daily schedule that was stipulated in the CDSPC's contract. A limit of four years' service in a Travelling Post Office had been introduced in 1890 but this was not applied to the H&K until about 1897 and it was decided at that stage that it would not apply to those who were already serving. In 1918, nearly half of the H&K establishment still comprised men who, provided they remained fully efficient, were entitled to "life" terms on the mail boat. Most of the postmen and clerks who were based in the GPO tended to live

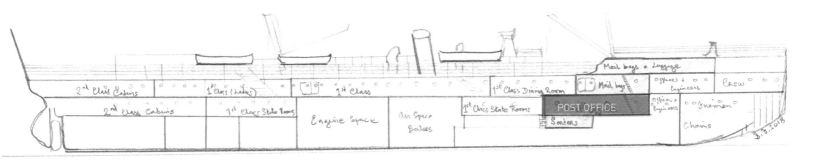

Sketch plan of the RMS *Leinster* based on designs signed by William Watson – Birkenhead 1 August 1895. The Post Office accommodation is highlighted. (Stephen Ferguson)

mails to the waiting London & North Western TPO carriage took about 15 minutes and then the train was on its way on its 264-mile journey to Euston station in London. It was usual for five of the dozen or so staff on the morning trip from Kingstown not to return on the afternoon boat but to continue their work as far as Crewe on the up TPO to London. At Crewe these sorters would get off and, about midnight, board the night TPO back to Holyhead. There, they would join the thirty-four sorters who had arrived on the night sailing from Kingstown and all would work the very heavy duties on the early morning mail boat from Holyhead so that Dublin mail would be ready for delivery on arrival. The whole operation was a remarkable lesson in precision-timing, co-operation between the sea and rail companies and commendable dedication on the part of the postal staff. A certain imaginative creativity was occasionally necessary to decipher some of the addresses, the author of one article on the mail boats reporting that the captain had been shown letters sent back by Irish emigrants, some containing hard-earned cash for their families, which were addressed in this rather inscrutable manner: 'to my mother in the white

cottage with the green door at the end of the village' or 'Betty McGuire at the house forninst the forge'.[20] The Postmaster General's reports of the time bear out such stories and today's Post Office staff still take pride in overcoming cryptic addressing challenges.

Sorting accommodation on the original *Leinster* and its sister ships had, with the increase of mail volumes, become inadequate despite successive modifications. The sorting office had originally been only 18 feet long but an additional 12 were added subsequently with three feet squeezed on in 1877 and about 10 more in 1883. The difficulty was that each expansion encroached on passenger space and, from the point of view of the CDSPC, there was an inherent tension between providing suitable space for the Post Office sorting staff and accommodation for paying passengers, especially first class passengers. The sorting office on the ships adjoined the first class sleeping cabins. When the *Ireland* joined the "Provinces" on the H&K route, she demonstrated some improvement in the facilities provided for the Post Office. The ship offered a sorting office which was 43 feet 9 inches long and 8 feet 1 inch

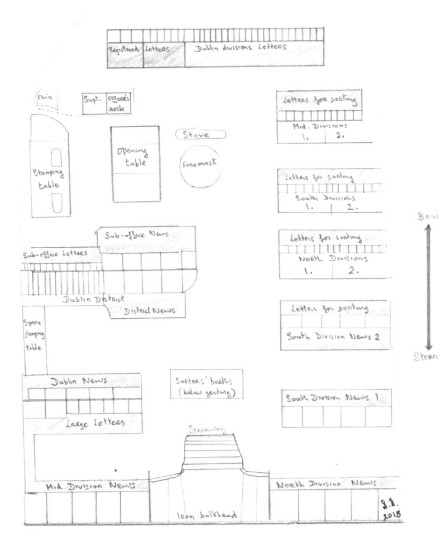

This sketch of the mail boat sorting office is based on the *Ireland's* layout but the design, with sections for registered letters and newspapers, opening and stamping tables and various sorting divisions would have been very similar on the *Leinster*. (Stephen Ferguson)

high. The nature of the ship meant that the space tapered in width fore and aft, the aft dimensions being 30 feet 9 inches but the forward width just 21 feet 4 inches. The mail bags were stored in a small locked mail shed, approximately 10 feet long by 12 feet wide, and there was further, larger storage space on the main deck under the shelter of the hurricane deck. There was not sufficient space for the bags to be held in the sorting office so the sorters would take down bags as they needed them, empty the mail onto the opening table and then proceed to sort the letters into the various onward divisions. The *Ireland* also provided sleeping accommodation, 24 berths, for the sorting clerks in a room that was 23 feet 6 inches long and tapered in width from about 28 and a half feet to just under 23 feet.

The *Ireland's* post office was used by the shipyard as the starting template for that in the 1896 Provinces. This is clear from the *Leinster's* contract document, similar to those used for the other Provinces.[21] It states that the ship's post office should be fitted out as in the *Ireland* but a little larger with suitable fittings and what was called a mail master's chair. Management and staff in Dublin had several improvements to put forward as discussion progressed. While the basic lay-out of the sorting office was satisfactory, increased sorting space was a priority. The down night mail brought the heaviest traffic with some 22 to 28 staff engaged in sorting about 60,000 items and making up about 120 bags for Irish towns on the voyage from Holyhead to Kingstown. The inspector who carried out the survey on the *Ireland* in January 1895 had no hesitation in reporting to London that space was insufficient, with four men sorting into

"Roads" or sorting boxes measuring only eight feet and having, consequently, to share each other's boxes. The man who had the misfortune to be standing nearest the side of the ship had barely room to move, the inspector noting that 'he may almost be said to stand on one leg owing to the narrow space and the curve in the side of the boat'. [22] The design of the new vessels and the abolition of paddle propulsion in favour of twin-screw ships would allow more width, it was felt, for the sorting office. There was no electric light in the old Provinces' sorting offices and the new contract provided an opportunity for the Post Office to look for this. The staff wanted better lavatory accommodation, a separate sleeping cabin for the officer in charge and improved arrangements for obtaining food and having their own food cooked.

Management specified that the new sorting offices should be 60 feet long and at least 5 feet wider than the *Ireland*. The locked mail shed was to be doubled in length and the covered accommodation for mail on the main deck was to be at least 850 square feet. Sleeping accommodation for staff was to be increased to 35 berths in a properly ventilated cabin. The H&K sorters, unlike their comrades on a later transatlantic RMS vessel, the *Olympic*, who said they were kept awake by 'low class Continentals' indulging 'through the silent hours…in singing and instrumental music', moved in very well-behaved company and had no complaint to make against the CDSPC's passengers![23] A mechanised system for transferring the mails was considered but rejected on the basis that it seemed, in respect of letters if not parcels, "very doubtful whether any system could be adopted which would not cause loss rather than gain of time". [24] Writing on 6 June 1894, H. L. Cresswell, the Secretary in Dublin, reminded London that a quicker voyage reduced sorting time and must mean more sorting staff if the same amount of work was to be handled. His overall view of the CDSPC was very favourable and, if the voice of the Irish Post Office were to have been the only one heard, the new contract would have been awarded to the Company much sooner than it was:

> *Their performance of the service has, in my judgement, left nothing to be desired…In their relations with the Post Office in Ireland they have always, with unfailing courtesy, shewn the fullest desire to meet the wants and wishes of the department and, in the event of any one of their tenders being accepted, I feel sure that complete confidence may be placed in the thoroness & efficiency with which they will carry out all that they undertake.* [25]

In the event, the Company had still a great deal of work to do to gain the contract but the sorting facilities on the new ships, when they entered service in 1896-7, were well up to Post Office expectations.

From the beginning, Post Office staff on the mail boats were given special H&K date stamps to cancel the postage stamps on the letters they were sorting and the dedicated philatelist takes pride in identifying the various types used during the 62-year period of on-board sorting. The ships' names never appeared in the date-stamps and until the start of the twentieth century particular date stamps were not allocated to the individual packet ships. The ship's initial, L for *Leinster* for instance, was introduced on a metal date stamp in

The L on this 1911 postmark identifies this datestamp as one used on the *Leinster*. (An Post Museum & Archive)

1902 and this makes it possible to identify which ship sorted which letters. A rubber date stamp, for use on parcel mails, was introduced in 1901. When the *Leinster* set sail on Thursday 10 October 1918 the sorting staff had taken on board 134 letter bags. In addition, they had a big consignment of parcels, a total of 354 parcel receptacles. Of these 327 had been made up in the GPO's Parcel Office in Dublin and the remaining 27 had come directly from the Great Northern Railway's night mail dispatch. Most of the mail was lost when the ship was sunk but S.G. Forsythe, the Secretary, told

London on the afternoon of the catastrophe that three bags and two sacks of "empties" had been recovered. These were probably the three bags made up for New York which, on 21 October, the Liverpool postmaster acknowledged receiving from Dublin. They had been salvaged by United States warships: the USS *Utah*, the USS *Dixie* and the USS *Bushnell* in the Irish Sea. In Liverpool, the bags were opened, the correspondence dried and censored and sent forward for delivery if this was possible. Another bag was found in the sea just off Portrane in north county Dublin and a reward of 5 shillings paid to the finder. A further bag was washed ashore on the Isle of Man in December. Claims against the Post Office in respect of contents lost in the mail on board the *Leinster* were subsequently charged against the German Government. Special postal markings or *cachets* were applied to some of the letters found and sent on for delivery through the postal system. These are scarce items and they generally bear just the simple legend 'Salved from S.S. "Leinster"', a sombre reminder of the sorting office staff and all those who lost their lives that day.

A tangible and poignant relic of the *Leinster* tragedy, this envelope was recovered from the sea and forwarded by the Post Office to its destination in Canada where it arrived on 12 November 1918, one day after the armistice was declared. Note the greatly understated casualty figure. (An Post Museum & Archive)

The First World War

Opposite page: Kingstown was a naval base as well as a packet station. This photograph shows early torpedo boats berthed opposite the mail boat pier. (Davisonphoto/ Chapman Livingston Collection)

For a time the Great War remained only a distant rumble for many Irish people. Its economic effects, in terms of food production and export and employment generally, were beneficial to Ireland and since conscription was never introduced here, the constant draining away of men to the front affected the country less than the rest of the United Kingdom. Of course, many men volunteered, especially in Ulster, and the standing British army had long comprised a higher than average proportion of Irishmen. Post Office men throughout Britain and Ireland were encouraged to "join the colours", as the phrase went, and there was even a specific Post Office regiment in the British army, the Post Office Rifles. Post Office telegraphists were in particular demand because of their technical knowledge and potential use in army communications work. The Post Office's routine work in the collection, sorting and delivery of letters was of vital importance too, in terms of the morale-boosting effects that correspondence between soldiers and their families so often provided. In all of this, the mail boats on the Kingstown-Holyhead route continued to play a vital role with Post Office staff working as usual below decks and passengers strolling the promenade decks above them.

From the outset of the war, Germany had made very effective use of its submarines in the seas around Britain and Ireland. Both warships and merchant ships were attacked but in the earlier part of the war it was German practice to allow passengers and crew aboard merchantmen to leave their ships before they were sunk. In an effort to counteract their success, Britain disguised warships as merchantmen – so-called Q-ships – and this was a factor in Germany's decision to declare, on 4 February 1915, a war zone around the British Isles within which merchant ships were sunk without warning. In September 1915, this unrestricted submarine warfare was suspended for a time, in response to pressure from the United States, but was resumed in February 1917. The tactic nearly succeeded in forcing Britain to seek terms, with more than 500 merchant ships sunk between February and April. The introduction of convoys, the use of aircraft and the deployment of new depth charge weapons, however, turned the tide in favour of Britain. By mid-1918 the German navy was suffering very high U-boat losses and by the autumn it had become clear that Germany could not win the war. The dwindling number of U-boats, however, maintained a desperate campaign in the face

Irish Guards receive letters from home. Letters to and from Irish soldiers were carried on the Holyhead mail boats, sorted in a huge sorting office in Regent's Park in London and sent on to the correct regimental locations at the front. (Irish Picture Library/Fr. FM Browne SJ Collection)

of imminent defeat and on 10 October, just two weeks before they were ordered to cease offensive operations and return to base, the RMS *Leinster* found itself in the sights of UB-123 under the command of its captain, Oberleutnant Robert Ramm.

While there had been a couple of close shaves, the CDSPC's ships had been fortunate in having had very few accidents over the many years they carried the mails. Indeed, Edward Watson, joint managing director and author of the Company's H&K history concludes his study with these prophetic words:

> *If the Almighty is pleased in the future to afford the Irish mail route the same immunity from really serious accidents as has been the case in the past, those responsible for the service, and the travelling public, will have every reason to feel most sincerely thankful.*[26]

He finished his book, however, before the outbreak of the war in 1914. The Company's general insurance policy, which covered risks of all kinds, was in force until April 1915 but from that date it had to pay an additional premium to cover war risks. The Post Office was approached on the subject and while it acknowledged that it had, in the eighteenth century, compensated mail boat contractors for loss or damage in war time, it pointed out that there was no provision for this in the current mail contract and the Postmaster General could not act as if there were. When the *Connaught* was requisitioned for war service in May 1915 the position was different, of course, and the Admiralty assumed responsibility for the ship which, in March 1917, would fall victim to a torpedo while working as a troopship in the English Channel. At the outset of the war the mail boats had been painted in "dazzle" camouflage colours which,

by presenting a disrupted pattern in submarine periscopes, made it more difficult, it was believed, for U-boat commanders to determine the direction and speed of their targets. Look-outs were posted to check for German submarines, and airships, operating from Wales but with a base also at Malahide Castle, were used to scan the seas below them. Damage to the airship docking mechanism at Malahide on the day before the *Leinster* was sunk may, indeed, have deprived her of a "blimp" escort the following day. The mail boats were instructed to pursue a zig-zag course which made it difficult for prowling U-boats to make ready and fire their torpedoes before a ship changed course. The Provinces were also very fast and the travelling public had confidence in their speed and ability to dodge

danger.[27] The Government and the navy were happy to encourage this misplaced optimism and consistently declined to provide a regular destroyer escort despite representations from the City of Dublin's directors who knew there had been several near misses.

On 7 April 1916, shortly before the mail boat was due to leave Kingstown, the captain received a message from the commander of the naval base, Captain Henry Aplin, instructing him not to leave the harbour because a submarine had been reported close to the ship's route. This was followed, a little later, by another telling him he could proceed to Holyhead as usual but that no lights, including navigation lights, were to be shown. He was told to keep a good lookout for submarines

The *Connaught* leaving Kingstown harbour. Requisitioned as a troopship, she would be sunk in the English Channel in 1915. (Davisonphoto/Chapman Livingston Collection)

and to make sure all passengers were warned before the ship departed that a submarine was in the vicinity. Such an instruction obviously posed severe difficulties for the CDSPC. There was a risk of collision if it sailed without navigation lights and a related risk that it might invalidate its insurance cover by so doing. It had an obligation under the mail contract to sail once the mails were on board and it feared that its passenger business would be damaged if there were to be regular delays attendant on Admiralty instructions. As Dubliners came to terms with the aftermath of the Easter rebellion at the start of May and local postal staff with the destruction of their GPO, officials in the Company, Admiralty and Post Office did their best to pass the buck in relation to this rather tricky issue. The naval authorities stated that the ships would not be allowed to sail if it was unsafe but that no absolute guarantee could be given on the question of submarines. The dangers of sailing

without lights might be largely reduced "by exercising reasonable and proper care and maintaining a good lookout", the Admiralty had advised the Post Office on 30 April. The Post Office, for its part, was prepared, following Admiralty advice, to regard a submarine warning as an exceptional circumstance under clause 17 of the mail contract, leave the decision to sail in the hands of the Company and its officers and exempt it from penalties arising from any consequent delay in sailing.

Edward Watson, joint managing director, and the Company's solicitor, T. F. Rider, met H. S. Carey, Second Secretary of the Post Office in London on 17 May to suggest that the Post Office should indemnify it against any loss sustained through sailing without lights on occasions when the Admiralty advised of the presence of enemy submarines. In a memorandum to the

Top: Many of the *Leinster's* victims are buried at Grangegorman military cemetery: the gravestones bear the emblems of many different nations. (Stephen Ferguson)

Right: This First World War Austrian post card, under the heading 'Sinking of an English steamer in the Irish Sea', seems to foretell the fate of the *Leinster*. (An Post Museum & Archive)

Postmaster General, the Post Office Secretary, Evelyn Murray, suggested that

> *The Company is evidently anxious not to incur odium through suspending the Mail Service on its own responsibility, and would be glad to be in a position to maintain the service without financial risk to itself or (failing that) to be able to say that the Government had acquiesced in the suspension.*[28]

He went on to say that if there were a real risk in sailing without lights, it would not be justifiable for the mail boat to put to sea, jeopardising passengers, crew and mails 'merely to avoid interruption to the service'. Decisions, he argued, had to be made by the Company in the light of local circumstances and the Post Office could offer no indemnity to it. Watson contemplated using his trump card, the influence of the Irish MPs, to take the matter further but agreed to accept the

Post Office decision. Day and night sailings of the mail boats continued to be operated until October 1918, a mere ten days before the *Leinster* was sunk, when the night service was suspended. The notice in the *Post Office Circular* of 24 September 1918 was brief and, under the heading Irish Mail Service, simply informed staff that the sailings of the H&K night packets would be 'modified' from 1 October 'so as to enable the voyages to be completed as far as possible in daylight' with the connecting night mail Up and Down TPO services between Holyhead and London also being suspended.

10 October 1918 –
'The most terrible thing I ever witnessed'

When William Birch, master of the *Leinster*, set sail from Kingstown just before nine o'clock on the morning of 10 October 1918 he had 771 people on board – a crew of 77, Post Office staff of 22, 180 civilians and 492 soldiers. Within a few hours, the Dublin-born captain and well over 500 of the *Leinster's* passengers would be dead, the memory of scores of men and women struggling in the water seared on the mind of one man who saw the results of the attack from another ship: 'It was the most terrible thing I ever witnessed in my life.'[29] The German U-boat commanders were aware that the *Leinster* and its sister ships were in 1918 regularly transporting troops and high-ranking officers. The *Leinster* carried troops only twice in 1917 but in 1918 it did so on over thirty occasions. The typical journal entry is 'embarking troops after mails and luggage on board'.[30] They also carried what the ships' journals refer to as 'naval luggage' and sometimes, more openly, as military equipment. It has been suggested that precision optical lenses, manufactured by the firm of Grubb in Rathmines and used in periscopes, may have formed part of this naval luggage.[31] In 1915 the ships, on Admiralty instructions, had been withdrawn from service and fitted with a gun at the Cammell Laird

shipyard. In the light of the information the Germans were able to collect, it is not surprising that their U-boat commanders had instructions to regard the mail boats as military targets. Not far from the Kish lightship, Captain Ramm of the German submarine, UB-123, was patrolling. Shortly before 9.45 a.m. he fired the first of three torpedoes at the ship. His first torpedo missed the target but the second one struck the ship's sorting office and was responsible, directly or indirectly, for the death of most of the Post Office staff. The sole survivor, J. J. Higgins, was seen later that day by the Controller of the Dublin Postal District, Henry Tipping, who said that, while the man was in no condition to write out a statement himself, he had explained what had happened to Tipping who made a note of it. Viewed from today's perspective it seems extraordinary that a man who had just survived such a traumatic tragedy and the loss of all his colleagues declined to go to hospital and simply got a lift on an army lorry back to the GPO where he borrowed an overcoat and went home. Higgins' eyewitness account of the event, recorded that very day by Tipping, is important and deserves to be quoted in some detail here.

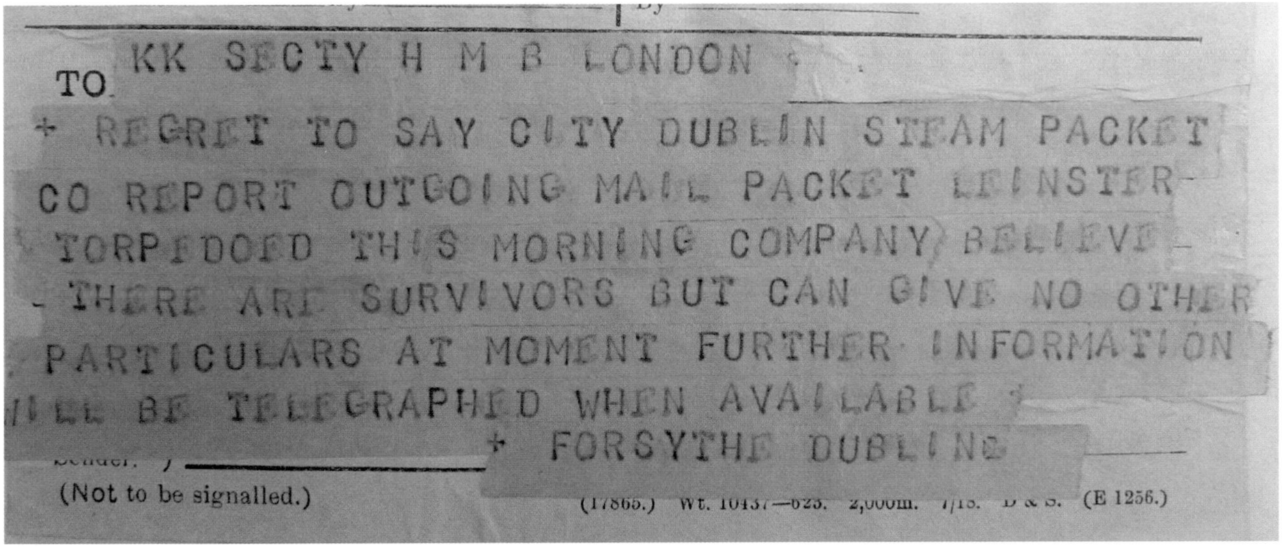

TO KK SECTY H M B LONDON +

+ REGRET TO SAY CITY DUBLIN STEAM PACKET CO REPORT OUTGOING MAIL PACKET LEINSTER TORPEDOED THIS MORNING COMPANY BELIEVE THERE ARE SURVIVORS BUT CAN GIVE NO OTHER PARTICULARS AT MOMENT FURTHER INFORMATION WILL BE TELEGRAPHED WHEN AVAILABLE +

+ FORSYTHE DUBLING

(Not to be signalled.) (17865.) Wt. 10437—623. 2,000m. 7/18. D & S. (E 1256.)

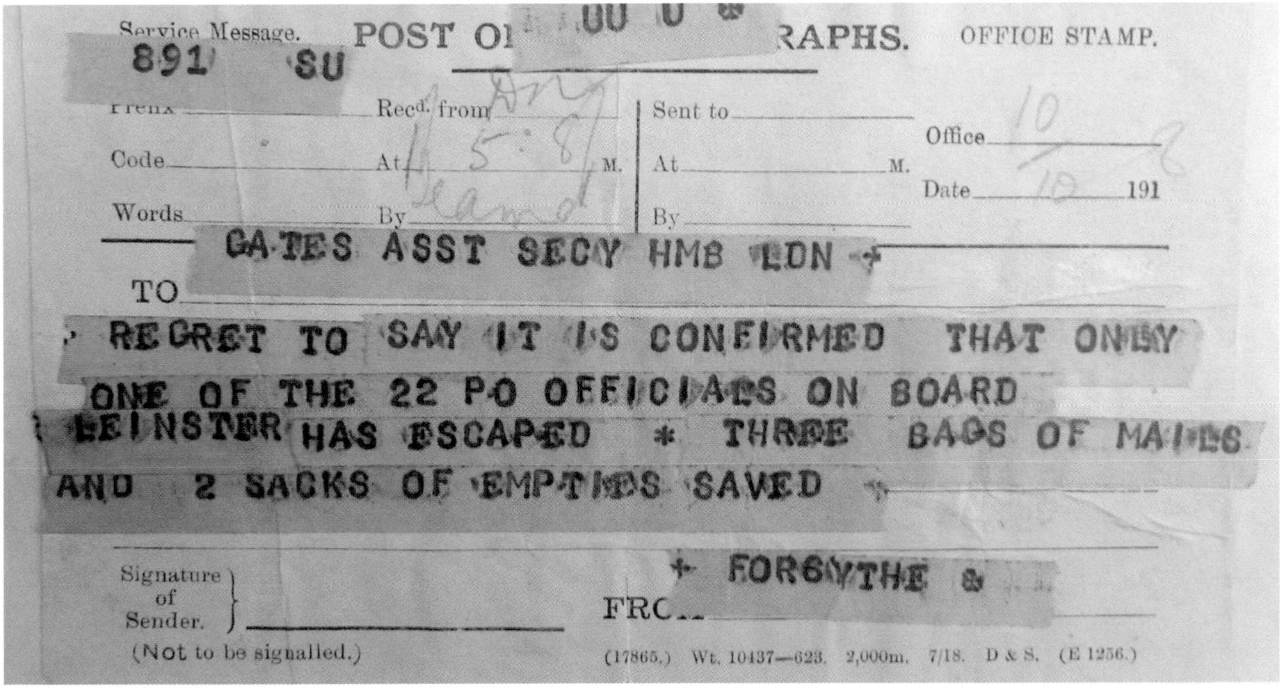

Service Message. POST OFFICE TELEGRAPHS. OFFICE STAMP.

891 SU

Prefix — Recd. from — Sent to — Office

Code — At 5·8 M. — At — M.

Words — By — By — Date 191

TO GATES ASST SECY HMB LDN +

REGRET TO SAY IT IS CONFIRMED THAT ONLY ONE OF THE 22 PO OFFICIALS ON BOARD LEINSTER HAS ESCAPED * THREE BAGS OF MAILS AND 2 SACKS OF EMPTIES SAVED +

Signature of Sender. + FORSYTHE +

FROM

(Not to be signalled.) (17865.) Wt. 10437—623. 2,000m. 7/18. D & S. (E 1256.)

Preserved on file one hundred years later, these are the telegrams that conveyed the terrible news of the *Leinster* disaster from the GPO in Dublin to Post Office headquarters in London. (© Royal Mail Group Ltd, Courtesy of The Postal Museum)

I was in the Registered Letter enclosure with Mr. Murphy and Mr. Attwooll when the torpedo struck the ship – I think it must have struck near the forward portion of the Sorting Office. Mr. Patterson was seated at his desk outside the Registered Letter enclosure. At the moment of impact all lights went out and except for a very faint glimmer from the port lights which were mostly under water the place was in darkness. Mr. Attwooll was standing nearest the door of the enclosure and I was next to him. I told him he had better get out but he made no answer. I passed by him and stept out into the Sorting Office and was immediately over my waist in water. I looked all round and saw none of my colleagues – I saw nothing but falling beams and twisted iron of the Sorting Divisions. I heard no sound but the roaring of water. I clambered over some bags in the centre of the office with the water rising higher as I advanced and reached the stairway with wood floating round my face. The stairway had entirely disappeared but there was light from the opening overhead. I struggled for the opening and caught some electric wires hanging from the roof and hauled myself up floating to the Mail shed.

It is worth remembering at this point that the post office sorting office, located below the water line, was two decks below the main deck of the mail boats. What was called the mail shed, where full bags of mail were stored, was one deck down and it was approached by two separate staircases, one at each end of the room. There was, however, only one staircase which led from the mail shed to the sorting office and it seems clear from Higgins's account of the disaster that it was destroyed by the explosion. Those postal staff who survived the initial blast of the torpedo were effectively trapped, a point which Tipping, in his report of 14 October to the Secretary, duly made, noting that the destruction of the stairway may have contributed to the loss of life amongst the Post Office staff. It was a danger, he added, that had been foreseen by the staff themselves and brought to attention earlier in the year.

Jack Higgins, however, was not the only man who had made it out of the sorting office as his account reveals. Having reached the main deck, via the intact mail shed stairs, he remembered there were life belts in the mail shed so he went back down again to get one. There, standing ankle deep in the sea water, he saw John Ledwidge emerging from the sorting office and he told him to get a life belt.

This he did and I tied it on him and tied my own – I did not think anyone could have got out of the Post Office after me. I next went amidships to look for a coat, as I had been working in shirt and trousers, but didn't get one. Coming forward again Mr. Ledwidge had hold of Mr. Bolster and was tying a life jacket on him. Mr. Bolster got me to take off his boots as one of his legs had been hurt in the explosion. He then jumped clear into the water and I did not see him again or Mr. Ledwidge.

Higgins saw one further member of the Post Office staff. He had swung himself down a rope and managed to get into a life boat. After shoving off from the *Leinster*, he looked up at the ship and

saw Mr. McDonnell on the deck and get out over the rails. Then the second torpedo struck the ship and I

Top: While his body was not recovered, the family gravestone in Mount Jerome cemetery bears witness to the death of Jennins Attwooll, one of the Post Office staff who died on the *Leinster*. (Courtesy of www. irishwarmemorials. ie)

Right: Limerick-born Samuel Forsythe, Secretary of the Irish Post Office, at the time of the tragedy. (An Post Museum & Archive)

did not see him again. The ship turned sideways and went down head first. I took an oar and after about two hours we were picked up by a destroyer.[32]

This is a measured, factual statement, tidied up a little perhaps by Tipping as he noted what he was hearing from the only man to have survived from the *Leinster's* postal staff, but it creates a powerful and lasting impression of the terrible moments immediately after the ship was struck by the torpedo. Jennins Attwooll doesn't reply to Higgins as he leaves the Registered Letter room – was he unconscious, in shock or badly hurt?[33] Tom Bolster, on duty in the same room, was injured but still able to make his way out of the Registered Letter office and escape up to the deck where John Ledwidge helped him put on a life jacket. There is no word from the Superintendent, Richard Patterson, at his desk just outside the Registered Letter enclosure. Alfred McDonnell also managed to escape to the main deck but he must have died when the second torpedo struck the ship. Attwooll, originally from England, left a wife and ten children and while his name is remembered on a family gravestone in Mount Jerome cemetery, it is believed his body was not recovered. Writing in a union magazine, *The Postal Worker*, eighteen years after the ship was sunk, Jack Higgins vividly recalled the destruction of the *Leinster's* post office and his abiding memory, up to his chin in water, was of "swimming through a sea of white letters" as he desperately sought a way to escape.

The rescue of survivors was co-ordinated by the naval authorities in Kingstown and patrolling destroyers and other vessels were sent to the aid of the stricken ship. Lifeboats had been launched from the *Leinster* but there was naturally a degree of panic and some regrettable incidents, particularly after the second torpedo struck the ship, which meant many people ended up in the sea. A wireless message, announcing that the ship had been attacked, was received at Kingstown but it remains unclear who sent the message. The signal was weak and the identity of the transmitting station was not made known. The *Leinster's* radio is thought to have been put out of action and it was suggested that the incoming *Ulster* sent the message. The *Ulster*, indeed, had passed the *Leinster* only a few minutes before the attack and some of its passengers may even have witnessed the first explosion aboard the *Leinster*. Wartime censorship and the refusal of the Government to release certain information after the event has made it very difficult to be sure exactly what happened immediately after the ship was torpedoed. It is unlikely now that the full story will ever be known and what we do know is the result of careful research by Roy Stokes, Philip Lecane and others who painstakingly pulled together evidence from the sources that were available.

Management in the GPO in Dublin first heard of the disaster at 10.50 that morning via a telephone message from the CDSPC and the Secretary, Sam Forsythe, immediately sent a telegram to London. It was not known, however, that the *Leinster* had definitely been sunk until about 2 p.m. and there was, for a time, a mistaken belief that the ship was still afloat

Top & right: The
Ulster at rest on
a calm day in
Kingstown in 1909
(Davisonphoto/
Chapman
Livingston
Collection) and her
journal record for
10 October 1918,
the day she passed
the outgoing
Leinster just
minutes before she
was torpedoed.
(Courtesy of the
National Library
of Ireland)

and that it might be possible to tow it back to Kingstown. As survivors were brought back to the harbour, this was shown to be untrue and the scale of the disaster and shocking loss of life numbed local people. By mid-afternoon, staff in the GPO feared that all but one of their colleagues had been lost on the mail boat and Forsythe contacted W. G. Gates, Assistant Secretary in London, at 4.15 p.m. with further information. He reported that the *Leinster* had sunk within 12 minutes of being struck by two torpedoes, some 12 miles off the coast and that, while not all survivors had been brought ashore, only one member of the Post Office staff had so far been saved.

Forsythe's other concern was what was to be done about the afternoon mail boat which was scheduled to sail at 2.30 p.m. He had been in touch with Richard Jones, Secretary of the CDSPC, and had been told that the Admiralty had closed the port and that the *Ulster's* captain was unwilling to sail without an escort. Forsythe then asked the senior naval officer at Kingstown if an escort would be provided and was told it would but that the timing of departure was uncertain. In the circumstances, he arranged for the mail and postal staff to be ready for departure and the *Ulster* duly left Kingstown at 3.11 p.m. with the mails but with no passengers. It is remarkable that, in the midst of this tragedy and amongst the chaos and grief of Kingstown that afternoon, the *Ulster* should have set sail so stoically. Not a word of objection was heard from the postal staff setting out on that ship even though the fate of their colleagues – in one case a brother-in-law – and so many others on board the *Leinster* was known. It must have been particularly hard for one young man, Daniel Smyth, who was a cabin boy on the *Ulster* and whose father Adam was one of the postal sorters feared lost. The postal service was, at that time of course, a vital part of communications infrastructure in a way that it no longer is and Post Office staff throughout the Department knew this but it in no way detracts from the calm courage with which the postal

staff and ship's crew faced departure that afternoon. They had a destroyer escort but no way of knowing whether one or more German submarines were lying in wait for them. Forsythe was proud of the packet staff that day and in his report to the Secretary in London made sure to put on record their loyalty and devotion to duty which, he said, deserved 'in circumstances which might have justified hesitation…the highest commendation'.[34] In the event, the *Ulster* arrived safely at Holyhead about 6.15 p.m., as reported by Thomas Kearney, the assistant surveyor on the North Wales district, who was able to confirm for the Home Mails Branch London that he had arranged for the waiting day mail bags to be immediately loaded on board the ship in readiness for her return voyage the following morning.

A fine view of the *Leinster* as she rounds the east pier on her way to Holyhead. (Davisonphoto/ Chapman Livingston Collection)

From the viewpoint of the Post Office the loss of the *Leinster* came at a particularly bad time since the CDSPC did not have a spare ship on hand to maintain the contracted twice-daily service between Kingstown and Holyhead: the *Munster* had been withdrawn by the Company for its periodic overhaul. Forsythe contacted the Company which told him that the *Munster* could be brought back into service at 24 hours' notice but that this would only be done with the consent of the Board of Trade and with the latter assuming complete responsibility for any breakdown or accident that might occur. Moreover, the CDSPC asserted that finding a replacement ship for the *Leinster* was actually a matter for the Admiralty since, at the time it had commandeered the *Connaught*, it had agreed to accept responsibility for the Company's obligations under the mail contract. It contended that since it was impossible to fulfil the terms of the contract without a third vessel, the Admiralty was under an obligation to find one. With the *Ulster* moored at Holyhead and no boat available in Kingstown for the morning service next day, Forsythe had to conclude that it would be possible to maintain only one daily service in each direction for the immediate future. In the circumstances, he proposed operating the night service only. E. A. Francis, one of the senior clerks in the Secretary's Office in London, had also been investigating the position and had already been in touch with the LNWR which confirmed that it would be able to assist if called upon. Consequently, by the close of business on 10 October, the Post Office had put emergency arrangements in place. The CDSPC would operate a night service only, leaving Kingstown for Holyhead at 2.30 p.m. and Holyhead for Kingstown at 7.00 a.m. The LNWR would help by taking over the next day's mails from Holyhead on its cargo ship to Dublin's North Wall and stood ready to take the Irish day mails on its passenger ship sailing from the North Wall at 12.30 p.m.

In the days immediately following the *Leinster's* sinking, the Post Office and the CDSPC tried to work out arrangements for re-establishing the normal twice-daily mail service. Forsythe thought about but was reluctant to put pressure on the Board of Trade to release the *Munster* before its overhaul had been completed. An approach to the Admiralty was also considered to see what obligations, if any, it had to the CDSPC following the loss of the ship. The requisitioning of a vessel based at Greenore or Fleetwood, to act as a temporary third packet ship on the H&K route, was discussed. Forsythe was also concerned about the safety of the sorting staff on the *Ulster* and *Munster* given that both ships,

like the *Leinster*, had only one entrance to and from the sorting office and the destruction of the stairs by the torpedo, he recognised, 'may have caused more loss of life than might have occurred.' It seems likely, indeed, that 18 of the Post Office's 22 staff died at their posts in the ship's sorting office. In the circumstances Forsythe contemplated the suspension of sorting on the ships altogether for the duration of the war. If the work were to continue, he wondered if the Admiralty would commit itself to the regular provision of an escort. On 14 October, the 2.30 p.m. afternoon sailing from Kingstown was delayed by the refusal of the ship's firemen to depart until an escort had been provided but the naval commander was unable, at first, to provide one. Questioned by the Kingstown postmaster, Barkeley Vincent, as to the reason for the delay, the commander stated that 'he could not divulge the reason'. The situation must have been rather tense for the commander went to speak to the firemen himself, after which he called in a destroyer and the mail boat eventually left at 5 p.m. with an escort of two destroyers and two airships. The same day Richard Jones, Secretary of the CDSPC, replied in unequivocal terms to Forsythe's enquiry as to what proposals the Company had for providing a replacement ship:

> *All responsibility in the matter is borne by the Admiralty, in the circumstances that Department is liable to supply a third vessel for the mail service, and on the 10th instant Mr. Watson was informed this would be done.*

Jones suggested that an LNWR boat, the *Duke of Cumberland*, which plied the Belfast to Fleetwood route would be the most suitable as it could steam at 19 knots and could be used on the day mail service until the *Munster* was ready to return to duty. In Holyhead on 15 October, the navy had made arrangements for naval ratings to act as firemen on the mail boat in case the CDSPC's staff refused to work but this proved unnecessary and the ship left as usual at 7 a.m. In an interesting aside, however, the Post Office's assistant surveyor there, telegraphed to London that 'Mr. Dillon and other MP's are interesting themselves in situation'. Writing to the Secretary in London on 15 October, Forsythe reported that

> *There have already been some defections from the Packet Sorting staff, which is not quite sufficient now for the proper manning of one service daily, & there is a danger of a complete break-down of the sea-sorting arrangements should uncertainty continue in regard to the matter of providing the vessels with a suitable escort.*[35]

Sorting on the mail boats was indeed suspended the following week. The Secretary of the Association of Irish Post Office Clerks wrote to the Postmaster General to express his concern and the PMG replied on 22 October to say that the matter would be kept under review and was, in keeping with similar suspensions in Great Britain, simply a measure brought about by wartime circumstances. Forsythe, who had earlier met a deputation from that union reported that, while the packet staff had drawn attention to the financial loss they would suffer they 'evidently preferred this to the daily risk of losing their lives though submarine attack'. A twice daily service was reinstated following completion of the *Munster's* overhaul. It resumed duty on the morning of 26 October when it conveyed the night mail from Holyhead and the *Ulster* took over the day mail service. In the absence of Post Office staff to look after the mail, the CDSPC expressed concern about their security but was informed by Forsythe that, in accordance with the mail contract, the master or commander of the mail boat was responsible for their safety. The overall picture over these few days is of men in various positions – the Post Office, the CDSPC and the naval bases at Kingstown and Holyhead – trying to cope with daily business in the midst of a wartime calamity, the scale of which was stretching resources.

The reaction:
many questions, few answers

Widespread public grief, shock and anger at the sinking of the *Leinster* were felt throughout Ireland. There were immediate practical matters for men in the CDSPC, the navy and the GPO to consider and it would not be long before political considerations too would begin to exert an influence on events. The *Times*, under the headline Irish Mail Boat Torpedoed, reported on 11 October that 500 people, including 20 of the 22 sorting staff, the captain and chief stewardess and Lady Phyllis Hamilton, who as a small girl had been present when her mother, the Duchess of Abercorn, had launched the *Ulster* back in 1896, were feared lost. It had, the writer said, 'stirred deep indignation in Ireland' and was 'the country's first real blow from German barbarity'. The suggestion that two of the postal staff had survived proved to be incorrect. The *Irish Times* spoke of the unspeakable agony of those who clung to wreckage as they waited an hour and a half or so to be rescued by the ships diverted to their location or dispatched from Kingstown to their rescue. On shore at the Victoria Wharf, volunteers from the Red Cross, the St. John Ambulance Brigade and other organisations waited to tend to the survivors with 'hot coffee, bovril and other suitable refreshments' and tenderly lift the bodies from the ships as they were

recovered. HMS *Lively* docked at 1.50 p.m. bringing in the bulk of the survivors, including J. J. Higgins, but more came ashore over the next couple of hours as HMS *Seal* and HMS *Mallard* came in to harbour. 'The people of Ireland', the *Irish Times* declared, had learned 'with a thrill of horror of the latest fiendish crime… committed almost at our very doors by the Germans'. King George V sent a message, relayed by the Lord Lieutenant: 'I am appalled to hear of this terrible disaster'. Alfred Blanche, French consul for Ireland, sent a special message to the GPO to express his profound sympathy and compassion for the postal staff who had perished in the *Leinster's* sorting office. They were, he went on, devoted public servants who had been engaged

The memorial plaque on the old Seamen's Institute building on Eden Quay. (Stephen Ferguson)

in the peaceful achievement of a task on which nowadays all our material, social and sentimental life is resting and they have died, in the execution of their duty, as true victims of the cause of humanity.[36]

James MacMahon, Irish Under Secretary and former Secretary of the Post Office in Ireland wrote to Forsythe in the GPO to express his sorrow at the loss of men, many of whom he had personally known, 'and all of whom I warmly esteemed and respected for their great courage and fidelity to duty.' Thomas Elliott, who had worked on the H&K packet until his move in 1912 to TPO duties in England, wrote to the secretary of the Association of Irish Post Office Clerks to express his shock at the death of his former comrades, men, he said, who had

met their end without fear in the cause of humanity – the same cause as the men in France are fighting for. They died, true Irishmen, upholding the finest traditions of their race.[37]

Lord French, the Lord Lieutenant, issued a statement praising the bravery of Captain Birch and the crew of the Leinster and recalling that 'throughout more than four years the Irish Mail packets have run unceasingly day and night' despite 'the constant and ever-present submarine menace'. They had died, he said, continuing in patriotic vein

as gloriously in the great cause as any sailor or soldier in the war, and the same applies to those devoted workers of the Postal Department who have also gone down at their post of duty.[38]

Much attention was given in all the newspapers to the *Leinster's* Post Office staff. The fact that all but one had died, the circumstances which, in a few cases, had led to last-minute switches on the duty roster, and a desire perhaps to highlight, in the context of such terrible destruction, the peaceful, ordinary work in which they were occupied, ensured there was much sympathy towards the GPO and its staff. The sorters who, for various reasons, had asked friends to substitute for them on that morning must have found it hard to cope with their feelings. Pasker was on duty in place of Aird, Archer in place of Curran and McDonnell had also covered for another man. The papers soon picked up on little details that added colour to their stories. Jennins Attwool left a widow and ten children behind him and was brother-in-law of Joseph Ingram, secretary of the Irish Railway Clearing Office. Two of his sons served in the army. Tom Bolster, Peter Daly and Michael Hogan had been keen GAA men, all three playing in the Davis Hurling Club which had a strong Post Office following. The *Irish Times*, in its commentary on 19 October 1918, noted that James Warbrook had been known as 'one of the few expert banjoists in Ireland'. Richard Patterson, the assistant superintendent who had been in charge of the *Leinster's* sorting office that day, also had an interest in sport: he was president and secretary of the Dolphin rowing club in Ringsend, not far from where he lived in Sandymount. Like Attwool, he also had sons in the army. Adam Smyth, notified only that morning, according to family remembrance, that he was to cover for a sick colleague, was in a rush and left his sandwiches in the kitchen at home. His daughter, Mary Clare, was sent after him with his lunch. That was the last time she would see her father. Behind the universal

Adam Smyth

Alfred McDonnell

Charles Archer

James Blake

James Warbrook

Jennins Attwooll

John Dewar

John Dolan

John Ledwidge

Joseph Bradley

Joseph Robinson

Matthew Brophy

Michael Hogan

Patrick Forbes

Patrick Murphy

Peter Daly

Richard Patterson

Tom Bolster

William Maxwell

William Pasker

William Wakefield

The twenty one Post Office staff who lost their lives on the RMS *Leinster*. See Appendix 1 for a little more information on these men and their dependants. (An Post Museum & Archive)

praise for the loyal and devoted men of the Post Office, than whom 'no more faithful or efficient men were to be found in the public service', would lie hidden memories of private personalities, friendships and enduring loss.[39]

While newspapers published official accounts of the disaster it was difficult, in the context of strict control of the press, for people to obtain more information in answer to the questions they had. Several Irish parliamentarians attempted to dig a little deeper, seeking to establish the facts through close questioning of the responsible Admiralty representatives in both the House of Commons and the House of Lords. Their questions emphasised the lack of regular protective escorts for the mail boats, attempted to find distinctions between the way the H&K ships and the Dover to Calais mail boats had been treated and drew attention to what seemed to be a peculiar twenty-five minute gap between the time of transmission and receipt of the *Leinster's* distress message. J. J. Clancy, MP for North County Dublin, asked the Secretary to the Admiralty whether, in light of the fact that destroyers were not able to keep up with the CDSPC's ships 'aeroplanes carrying depth charges could be employed as escorts'.[40] In his reply, T. J. Macnamara, the Canadian-born son of an Irish soldier and the Parliamentary and Financial Secretary to the Admiralty, pointed out that the real difficulty on the day of the tragedy had been the weather and that this would have prevented aircraft as well as destroyers from providing an escort. The comment is an interesting one for the seas were rough that day and at speed the navy's destroyers, which lacked the protective turtle-back decks of the mail boats, were liable to suffer some damage. There were occasions, indeed, when the latter were reported to have

outstripped their naval escorts, criss-crossing the bows of the destroyers as they pursued their zig-zag course across the sea. Such stories, however, need to be treated with some caution as it suited the Admiralty to emphasise the speed of the *Leinster* and its sister ships. John Dillon, MP for East Mayo and leader of the Irish Parliamentary Party, suggested that there was less protection for the Irish mail boats than there was for the English Channel ships but Macnamara successfully countered this when he recalled for the House the loss of no less than three channel mail boats, the *Queen*, *Normandy* and *Sussex*, none of which had been under convoy or immediate escort when they were sunk. The escort question was one which also drew observations in the House of Lords, the Earl of Mayo making the point that undermined the Admiralty's argument that the weather was too rough for a destroyer escort. "My experience", he said,

> is that even in fine weather there is no escort. I cross over pretty often, and the only times I have seen an escort were in one case a dirigible balloon, and in the other case, in fine weather and on a dark night, a destroyer was dodging in front of the mail boat. In Ireland we complain that there has never been sufficient escort for these boats in rough or in fine weather.[41]

The mail boats' journals do record occasional escorts, both destroyer and airship, before the sinking of the *Leinster* but there is also the frequent observation 'no escort seen on passage'. Lord Oranmore commented that he had travelled on the *Leinster* just two days before it was sunk and had been told then by a member of the crew that there had been an attempt to torpedo her the previous day. Feeling in Ireland would certainly have been strongly behind the Earl of Donoughmore's plain words when he said that

> there is an impression…that over this business someone has blundered, and we feel that we want a strong assurance that that blunder will not be repeated. There can only be one place in which the blunder has occurred. It has not occurred through the officials of the company. Ever since January, 1915, the company have been appealing to and urging upon the Admiralty that while they have been responsible themselves for the running of the mail boats…their strongest opinion has been that they have not been sufficiently protected. Their view has not been accepted by the Admiralty, and therefore the responsibility is upon the Admiralty for what has occurred….I have been informed of four occasions when a torpedo was fired at the mail boat and missed it. Surely that was enough to warn somebody responsible that, whatever the steps were that were being taken, they were likely to prove insufficient some day; and some further steps could have been taken. [42]

The other matter which received close examination was the transmission of the *Leinster's* distress message. At this stage, it is impossible to be quite sure of the sequence of events: there are discrepancies over times and the recollections of those who survived the disaster do not agree in all respects so it cannot be known now just how the message made its way to the naval commander in Kingstown. While there is certainly a suggestion of, at least, inattention at Kingstown we are not in a position to ascertain all the facts. Dr. Macnamara seemed to be less than comfortable replying to questions from Sir Robert Houston, a ship owner and

MP for Liverpool West Toxteth. On 23 October Houston asked whether, at the time the *Leinster* was sunk

> the wireless installation at Kingstown was out of order and did not receive the S.O.S. calls; and whether, although many Government craft, including destroyers, were in Kingstown harbour at the time the "Leinster" was sunk about 12 miles only from the harbour, a considerable time elapsed before any Government vessel reached the scene of the disaster.[43]

Richard Hely-Hutchinson, 6th Earl of Donoughmore, caricatured here in a *Vanity Fair* cartoon, was representative of the support enjoyed by the CDSPC from many Irish peers and MPs. (Courtesy of the Board of Trinity College Dublin, the University of Dublin)

An SOS message, Macnamara had informed the Commons the previous week, was sent at 9.25 a.m. on 10 October, perhaps in a very weak or garbled format from the *Leinster's* damaged equipment, but not received by the senior naval officer at Kingstown until 9.50 a.m. It should consequently have been with him within a minute or so. Houston goes on to state that the rescuing craft only arrived on the scene at 10.40 a.m., an hour and a quarter after the message was sent. Macnamara's reply on this occasion is simply that the message times had been correctly stated (although the 9.25 a.m. time for the sending of the message is very much at odds with other information and can hardly be right) and that all available vessels at Kingstown left within ten minutes. Perhaps the *Leinster's* message was so broken that it took time for it to be pieced together and understood but one has a sense that there may perhaps have been some slip-up on the part of the naval authorities at Kingstown. There is evidence to suggest that the *Leinster's* wireless had been damaged by the first torpedo explosion and that no message could consequently have been sent. On the other hand, there was also mention of an emergency wireless set and the fact that the *Leinster's* radio officer, Arthur Jeffries, seems to have died at his post. According to the *Freeman's Journal* of 29 October, the *Leinster* was able to send out only 'a very faint signal which the 'Ulster' picked up'. She then sent on a general SOS. It is curious though that the *Ulster's* journal makes no reference to this. There were also British naval patrol ships in the Irish Sea which may have passed on a message to Kingstown. At the brief inquest that was eventually held into the disaster, the Admiralty seems, according to the memory of the ship's purser, Bill Sweeney, to have

wished to muddy the waters a little on the question of timing. Such is the general lack of clarity here that there is even a possibility, cautiously advanced by Roy Stokes in his book, that Captain Ramm of UB-123 surfaced briefly and sent out the short humanitarian message, '*Leinster* torpedoed'. Since Ramm and his crew themselves died in a minefield soon afterwards, that speculation and the question of why he launched another torpedo, when it was clear the ship had already been struck, will remain unanswered.

It fell to T. J. Macnamara, Parliamentary Secretary to the Admiralty, to defend the Government's position in relation to the *Leinster*. (Courtesy of the Board of Trinity College Dublin, the University of Dublin)

TAKE UP THE SWORD OF JUSTICE

For army recruiting agents the loss of the *Leinster* no doubt brought to mind again the potential of this strikingly effective recruitment poster, issued after the sinking of the *Lusitania* in 1915. (An Post Museum & Archive)

of the sea: in his heart he might have known too that in wartime, the captains of merchantmen were under strict Admiralty orders not to stop to rescue the victims of ships that had just been torpedoed by a submarine. It was an order that defied the normal rules of the sea and the unspoken instinct of the seaman but fear of the enemy below the waves created yet another wartime inhumanity.

In the days following the disaster, opportunity was unashamedly taken by the Government to leverage public outrage in favour of the war effort. Strict censorship, of course, was imposed on press reporting and the public at that time had no exposure to the immediacy of digital channels which offer us both truth and lies with such extraordinary rapidity today. Germany was blamed for a dastardly and cowardly attack on a passenger vessel and its role in the deaths of so many innocent women and children was uniformly condemned. The captain of the U-boat which had sunk the *Leinster* should, if caught, be tried for murder, said one MP. In one speech, the Foreign Secretary, Arthur Balfour, was happy to perpetrate the myth that the *Leinster* served no military purpose and had been torpedoed in yet another simple manifestation of German brutality. There was no mention of the soldiers on board or the vessel's regular role in conveying unspecified military stores which are recorded in the ship's journals. Local Kingstown people must have known that the mail boats carried many soldiers as passengers but the official coverage is completely silent on the point. Irish MPs also must have known but it was the Cavan-born Thomas Lough, MP for Islington West, who raised the matter in the House of Commons on 15

Questions were asked as to why the *Ulster* and another LNWR ship had not gone to the aid of the *Leinster's* victims but the Deputy Speaker of the Commons prevented discussion on the point. 'That does not arise', he said, to which the MP for Limerick City, Michael Joyce, curtly replied 'Go to sea and learn something'. Joyce had himself been on the stricken *Leinster* that morning and had been rescued. A seaman in his earlier life, he had survived no less than four previous shipwrecks so, more than anyone, he knew the terrors

October when he asked the Admiralty representative

> *Is the right hon. gentleman aware that large numbers of officers and men are carried on these boats, and will he not promise to extend the same care with regard to the convoying of these troops as is given in other spheres of the War?*

He received no reply to his question. It is important to remember too that the particular nature of Irish politics made it vital for the Government to step delicately around certain matters. Conscription, which had not been applied in Ireland, remained a controversial issue and, while many Irishmen had voluntarily joined the British army, recruitment levels in some parts of the country were considered in army circles to be unacceptably low. Attempts in 1918 to link progress on Home Rule with the imposition of conscription and one curious plan, favoured by the Irish Chief Secretary, Edward Shortt, to encourage Irishmen to join the French army, came to nothing and tended to overlook the growing public shift towards a more republican form of nationalism. The army was quick to sense a recruiting opportunity in the mail boat's sinking and recruiting offices, despite the fact that the war was clearly drawing to a close, were speedily set up in Kingstown and in Dalkey. Some people certainly would have agreed with the sentiments expressed by one man in a letter written a couple of day after the sinking: 'The Leinster outrage shd. shame Irish men into the uniform if there is any sense of responsibility left.'[44] The *Irish Times*, taking a similar line on the day after the sinking, mentioned the 'brave Postal servants who now have found a true soldier's death' and went on to suggest that

> *At least one ray of light will gild the darkness of yesterday's tragedy if 'Remember the Leinster' becomes for young Irishmen today what 'Remember Limerick' was for their fighting ancestors on the battlefields of Europe.*

There were, however, some dissenting voices to this less than subtle approach and the *Freeman's Journal* of 12 October took exception to the "mischievous slanders" perpetrated by the Recruiting Council in its attempt to pin 'blood guilt on the men of Ireland'. One interesting leaflet, *The Leinster Outrage,* in the National Library's collection is clearly propagandist in tone but pertinently draws attention to the *Leinster's* role as a troopship and suggests circumstances were not quite as portrayed in newspaper reports.

Calls for a full public enquiry into the sinking of the *Leinster* were voiced in Parliament immediately after the event. John Dillon asked the Irish Chief Secretary to institute an 'immediate and searching inquiry…into all the circumstances connected with the sinking of the city of Dublin mail boat "Leinster"' and wanted the terms to be so drawn

> *as to permit of a full investigation into the communications which have passed during the last year between the City of Dublin Company and the Admiralty, in regard to the necessity for protecting the Holyhead mail packets, and the representations which have reached the Admiralty from other quarters on this matter*[45]

The Government declined to accept this suggestion and would maintain a steadfast opposition to the idea despite repeated calls for a full enquiry into the *Leinster* disaster. On 6 February 1919, Henry Campbell, the town clerk of Dublin Municipal Council, wrote to the Postmaster General to inform him that the council had adopted the following resolution:

> *That, having regard to the delay of Government in dealing with the question of the loss of the Royal mail Steam-ship 'Leinster' and five hundred lives, this Council hereby demands that the Government forthwith hold a public and impartial inquiry into the entire circumstances, and also into the case of each individual passenger lost.*[46]

Previously, the Government had advanced the view that any such enquiry would provide useful information to the enemy and was not consequently in the public interest. This was certainly a defensible argument in war time but the Government was, with experienced adroitness, able to adjust the argument for peace time circumstances by stating that 'no really useful purpose would be served now by setting up an inquiry in to the loss of the ship.'[47] There had, soon after the tragedy, been inquests into the deaths of two of the people who had lost their lives on the ship but the coroner kept a very tight grip on proceedings and neither the Admiralty nor the War Office attended. The inquest came to the unremarkable conclusion that Mr. John Shaw Jones and Miss Georgina O'Brien met their death by drowning and that both the CDSPC and the Kingstown naval authorities had done their best to save lives. The only controversial note sounded was the finding that an escort should have been provided to the *Leinster* that day. Some interesting information about the final moments of the *Leinster* did come to light from witnesses during the inquests but there were contradictions and ambiguities there too and these, without the participation of the responsible Government and naval personnel, remain unanswered. The inquest reported a finding of 'wanton destruction of innocent persons'. Edward Watson, managing director of the CDSPC since the death of his brother in March, said that the Company had been feeling the responsibility of the Irish Sea crossings since 31 January 1915, the occasion of the first torpedo attack. Without the Post Office decision to switch to daylight only sailings, just over a week before the disaster, he said he felt there would have been no lives saved at all. A few days after the inquests, the directors of the CDSPC presented their half-yearly report and commenting on the *Leinster*, deplored the terrible loss of life and briefly recounted the circumstances. They were quite clear that, in their view 'the disaster is one that need not have occurred' and that no effort on their part had been wanting in seeking adequate protection for the mail packets. In what may perhaps be taken as an additional oblique criticism of Government, they said that at the time the ship was struck by torpedoes, 'No patrols were sighted and a considerable time elapsed before rescue arrived.' It was their hope that 'the whole matter may be fully and searchingly investigated by an impartial tribunal.'[48]

Relief measures

While shock, grief and outrage dominated feeling in Ireland after the loss of the *Leinster*, attention also turned quickly to ways in which the families of those who had died might be given practical help. The great majority of victims had been soldiers drawn from the United Kingdom and its allies. Their dependants, in respect of pensions, were covered by the terms of their military service. There was discussion in Parliament of the plight of the families of the *Leinster's* crew and a desire to assist them. They too were covered under the pension regulations that applied to merchant seamen. The public at large was keen to contribute to relief measures and to this end the Lord Mayor of Dublin set up a relief fund which reached over £100,000. Private charitable events like musical evenings and sales of work also raised money for the victims of the disaster.

The Post Office was quick to respond to the need for financial assistance. On the day after the sinking, Tipping, Controller of the Dublin Postal District, had written to Forsythe with a proposal to relieve the immediate needs of the Post Office families affected and an official fund, started by Sorting Office staff, was established. This was the Post Office "Leinster" Disaster Fund, a fund specifically created in aid of the dependants of the Dublin postal staff who had lost their lives whilst performing their duty on the mail boat. It drew on the precedent of the 1907 Shrewsbury mail train derailment when three postal sorters had died. The managing committee, made up of senior Irish Post Office and Union officials, wrote to post offices and administrative divisions throughout Ireland and Britain appealing for contributions to the fund so that provision might be made for the widows and orphans. Of the twenty-one men who died, nineteen were married and they left behind over one hundred orphans, most of whom were young children. 'The Committee' felt it unnecessary 'to enlarge upon the distressing circumstances' but confidently relied on its correspondents 'to bring the movement to the notice of your Staff and upon your co-operation with them to make the Fund a success.' The appeal met with widespread and generous support from staff everywhere –£6 collected in Aberdare in Wales, £4 from Dundee in Scotland, £79 in Liverpool (including £20 from the Choral Society) and £680-4-7 from Dublin subscriptions. James MacMahon, who had been Post Office Secretary in Dublin before his promotion to

Report and Statement of Accounts

OF THE

Post Office "Leinster" Disaster Fund

IN AID OF THE

Dependents of the Dublin Postal Staff who lost their lives whilst performing their duty through the torpedoing of the Mail Steamer "Leinster", on 10th October, 1918.

In presenting the following statement showing particulars of subscriptions to and disbursements of the Fund, we desire on behalf of the Committee, to record our appreciation of the prompt organisation by members of the various classes of the Dublin Postal and Telegraph Staffs, of the movement to raise a Fund to provide for the widows and orphans of the Postal victims, as this timely organisation enabled the Committee to afford relief in cases of distress which required immediate alleviation.

We also desire to express our gratitude to the Postmasters and other Heads of Departments and Service Organisations throughout the United Kingdom for their active co-operation which produced such highly satisfactory results.

We tender our sincere thanks to all the subscribers and are glad to be able to state that the munificent contributions received in response to the appeal, in addition to the liberal sum received from the Dublin Mansion House Fund, enabled the Committee to give substantial relief to the widows and orphans.

The total number of dependents to be provided for was 113, and the disbursements have been made on the following basis, viz.,

Widows, £225 each.
Children under 8 years, £75 each.
Children 8-15 years, £45 each.
Children 16-20 years, £30 each.
Dependents of unmarried victims, £75 each.

In the cases shewn against the letters K. & T., the next-of-kin were not entitled to the benefits of the Superannuation Act of 1909 and the Committee awarded, in addition to the grant on the basis referred to, the equivalent of the gratuity in each case which would be payable under that Act. An additional sum of £100 was allowed in the case of "S" owing to two dependents incapacitated from employment through ill-health having to be provided for.

After disbursement of the main Fund as indicated above the amount remaining on hands admitted of a supplementary grant of £13/2/4 to each of the 21 families, and a final distribution has been made accordingly.

H. J. TIPPING, *Controller, Dublin Postal District.*
J. NORMILE, *President Irish Post Office Clerks Association.*
E. W. MAHON, *Hon. Secretary, District Council Postmen's Federation.*
C. G. PANTON, *Inspectors' Association.*
J. J. KENNY, *Controller, Dublin Telegraphs.*
L. W. KENNEDY, *Secretary Engineers' and Stores Association.*
J. R. HANRAHAN, *Clerical Assistants' Association.*
M. A. DUNNE, *Women Clerks' Association.*
WM. KILLEEN, *Chairman.*
J. McMANUS, *Hon. Secretary.*
J. POWER, *Hon. Treasurer.*

The Post Office 'Leinster' Disaster Fund was generously supported by postal staff throughout Ireland and Britain and payments from the fund helped alleviate immediate financial worries for dependants. (An Post Museum & Archive)

Under Secretary in Dublin Castle, gave three guineas while in Kingstown Mrs. Kearney's intriguing "Cushion Sweep" collected £4-5-9. The Lord Mayor's general Mansion House fund also made a very generous contribution of £5760 to the particular Post Office fund so that by the time the final accounts were published a year later a total of £9525-9-0 had been distributed to the 21 families. The money was distributed to the 113 dependants on the following basis:

Table 3 Post Office "Leinster" Fund – distribution of relief

Widows	£225 each
Children under 8 years	£75 each
Children 8-15 years	£45 each
Children 16-20 years	£30 each
Dependants of unmarried victims	£75 each

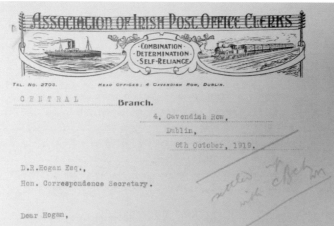

At a time of increasing political tension, the failure of the London-based Post Office Relief Fund to make payments on behalf of the *Leinster's* postal staff was seen as discriminatory by its Irish members. (Courtesy of the Irish Labour History Museum)

The special circumstances that applied to a few dependants who were severely incapacitated or ineligible for normal superannuation benefits were also taken into account by the Committee. Carefully and efficiently administered with just over £30 spent on printing, cheques and postage, the working of this relief fund is a model that could be followed today.

There was, however, some disagreement about the operation of another separate fund, the Post Office Relief Fund, which had been set up at the start of the war 'to alleviate distress among the dependants of Post Office Servants who joined the Colours or lost their lives in the War'. This fund, administered in London but with an Irish Branch committee, paid out death gratuities of £5 to each widow and £1 to each dependant. Application was duly made on behalf of the *Leinster* postal victims but a response from London was very slow in coming. Eventually, on the 24th April 1919 a letter was sent to Sam Forsythe in Dublin informing him that the Committee had recently met and had decided that 'they would not be justified in paying the Death Grants asked for.' The reason given was that a separate fund had already been set up for the 'special and exclusive use of the families affected through the torpedoing of the steamer.' This, unsurprisingly, went down very badly in Ireland where members of the Irish Branch of the PORF felt they had been placed in an invidious position in relation to Irish members who contributed to the fund. It was felt that the decision was discriminatory and, while the *Leinster's* postal staff had not joined the army, they had quite clearly died as a consequence of the war – Lord French himself had said as much immediately after the catastrophe – and ought to have been afforded the same treatment as other Post Office staff. The case of an English postman who had died during German bombardment of an English coastal town and whose claim had been admitted was cited in favour of the *Leinster* men but the appeal was disregarded. In the circumstances, the Association of Irish Post Office Clerks, the union which represented the SC&Ts who had died on the ship, called on its members to withhold their subscriptions from the fund in protest at the decision taken in London. It was, as the anniversary of the *Leinster's* sinking drew near, an unfortunate situation. The war was over but the situation in Ireland was tense and the Post Office and its staff were not exempt from the wider influence of politics. Happily, the fund, which following the war had difficulty meeting the disbursements paid out, was reinvigorated in 1925 when the newly independent Irish Post Office took on the responsibility of collecting subscriptions to finance the c£1,100 paid out annually to postal staff in the Saorstát.

While nothing came from the assets of the Post Office Relief Fund, dependants were entitled to and received pensions and gratuities in accordance with the Injuries in War (Compensation) Act 1915 and the Superannuation Act (1909). Widows and dependant parents were entitled to life pensions while children received payments until they reached the age of sixteen. Interestingly enough, the Association of Irish Post Office Clerks, writing on behalf of the staff who worked on the mail boats, had written to the Postmaster General in November 1917 seeking clarification on the application of these regulations which, in light of the additional allowances earned by the mail boat staff, offered, it felt, 'inadequate compensation to officers of the Holyhead and Kingstown packet.' The Association's main concern was to confirm that staff and their dependants would also receive their standard entitlements under civil service pension rules in the event of their being injured on the mail boat. On 25 October 1919 the Accountant in Dublin was asked to provide details on the sums paid out and the actuarial valuations so that the money might be included in the war reparations to be demanded from the German Government as part of the treaty of Versailles. He calculated a total sum of £36,781. The

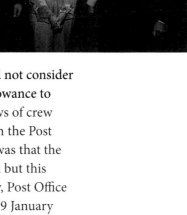

question of paying a special war risk allowance to postal staff on the mail boats had been raised in the House of Commons on 21 October 1918 but the Postmaster General replied that 'special provision' had already been made by means of the Injuries in War regulations and he did not consider further provision in the form of a risk allowance to be called for. Possible claims by the widows of crew members were raised by the Treasury with the Post Office in December 1919. The argument was that the Post Office had obliged the *Leinster* to sail but this was quickly rejected by Sir Evelyn Murray, Post Office Secretary, who pointed out in his reply of 9 January 1920, that at no stage had the CDSPC suggested the ship might not sail and, even if it had, Admiralty advice on potential dangers would not have been overruled by the Post Office. Murray saw no ground on which the Postmaster General should compensate the CDSPC for the loss of the *Leinster* nor, in fairness, had the Company proposed any such measure. The ship was nearly 20 years old and had been written down to close to scrap value. It had been lost in Government service and would be replaced, he believed, by the Admiralty or the Shipping Ministry.

Descendants of the *Leinster*'s Post Office staff were present at the unveiling of a commemorative plaque in Dún Laoghaire post office in 2003. A similar plaque may be seen in Dublin's GPO. (An Post Museum & Archive)

SAORSTÁT ÉIREANN

IRIS an PUIST

| Uimhir 32. | Dia Céadaoin | 7 adh lá Mí na Márta, 1923 |

Long Puist Ceibí agus Dún Laoghaire.
Deireadh le Sórtáil ar Sheirbhís Lae.

Cuirfear deireadh leis an sórtáil a deintear anois fa long puirt an Seirbhír Lae ag teact is ag imteact tar éis an 10adh lá Márta, 1923.

Toisc gur cuireadh an acló Port Oróce bóčar Iarann na hÉireann Suar, ní deintear málaí suar fé látair do'n long puirt ag Oifigí Tuata Éireann, agus ní beid gád le haon airčniú ar na cupamaca atá ann fé látair, act amáin ag Baile áta Cliat agus ag Dún Laogaire, agus tá teagairc rpeiriálta dá gcur go dtí rna hoirigí reo. Cuirfar amac fa gnát fige a tuile teagorc ar an deimniú a tabarfar irteač go generálta nuair a tornócard Port Oróce na mbótar Iarann air.

Ní déanfar suar aon portanna i long puirt an Lae tar éis an 10adh lá Márta.

Ag tornú leis an 12adh lá Márta déanfar suar málaí i bPort Bóčair Iarann Lonndun agus Ceibí do rna hoirigí reo mar leanar, le teact anall ar long puirt an Lae go hÉirinn.

An bóčar Iarann ó Tuaid.	An bóčar Iarann Tear is Tiar.
Droicead áta	Catair Dún Iarcais.
Dún Dealgan	Ceatarlac
Leitir Ceanann	Cluam Meala
Port an Dúnám	Inir
(le cófreagairt do'n Tuairceart generálta)	Mainirtir Fear Muige
	Cill Dara
	Cill Comnig
	Cill áirne
	Cill Moceallóg
	Mag Ealla
	Port Laoigire
	Nár Laigean
	Aonac Urmuman
	Cúil an tSúdaire
	Ror Cré
	Dúrlar Éile
	Tiobrard Árann
	Tráiglí
	An Tulac Mór
	Port Láirge

Holyhead and Dún Laoghaire Mail Packet.
Discontinuance of Sorting on Day Service.

The sorting which is now performed in the Mail Packet on the Day Service in both directions will be discontinued after the 10th March, 1923.

Owing to the temporary suspension of the Irish Up Night Mail trains, bags for the Day Packet are not now being made up at Irish Provincial Offices, and, except at Dublin and Dún Laoghaire, to which Offices special instructions are being sent, no change in existing despatches will, therefore, be necessary at present. Further instructions as to the vouching to be introduced generally, on the resumption of the Night Mail trains, will be issued in due course.

No mails will be made up in the Day Boat after the 10th March.

Mails for the undermentioned Offices will, commencing on the 12th March, be made up in the London and Holyhead T.P.O. for conveyance by the Day Boat to Ireland :—

Great Northern Line.	Great Southern and Western Line.
Drogheda	Cahir
Dundalk	Carlow
Letterkenny	Clonmel
Portadown	Ennis
(to contain correspondence for North generally)	Fermoy
	Kildare
	Kilkenny
	Killarney
	Kilmallock
	Mallow
	Maryborough
	Naas
	Nenagh
	Portarlington
	Roscrea
	Thurles
	Tipperary
	Tralee
	Tullamore
	Waterford

This 7 March 1923 issue of *Iris an Phuist*, the internal circular introduced after Irish independence, announced the end of daytime sorting on the mail boats. (An Post Museum & Archive)

Epilogue

⋯◦○◦⬩⬦━━━━━━━━

Kingstown : Alteration of Name.

On and after the 1st April the Kingstown Head Office will be known by the name " Dún Laoghaire." The change involves an alteration in the designation of the Holyhead and Kingstown Packet, which will be known as the " Holyhead and Dún Laoghaire Packet." The heading of letter bills enclosed with Mails for the Packet should be altered accordingly.

As Ireland in 1919 slipped into political turmoil and violence and then, with independence, moved towards the creation of its own identity, there was little appetite for remembering a mail-boat tragedy that occurred in the last month of the Great War. The loss of life had been dreadful but most of the victims had not been from Ireland and the vast majority, indeed, had belonged to the British army. In the changed circumstances of post-independence Ireland, the RMS *Leinster* and the mail boat connection were, in some respects, an embarrassing anachronism. The Dublin-London communications axis was no longer relevant and memories of an elegant ship and the people who travelled on her were uncomfortable perhaps. There was also misunderstanding of the true

The name Kingstown had been officially changed to Dún Laoghaire in 1922. (An Post Museum & Archive)

scale of the disaster, what one authority has called a 'huge understatement of casualties', because the official source did not count military deaths.[49] Kingstown itself would disappear from the map, remembered only in the archaic usage of those who hankered a little after the *ancien régime,* while Holyhead would continue to be the gateway for the thousands of Irishmen and women heading for London and the Percy French promise of digging for gold in the street.

For the City of Dublin Steamship Company the loss of the *Leinster* was a blow from which it did not recover. Application was duly made to the Government for a replacement ship but, as in the case of the *Connaught,* circumstances did not favour a timely and effective response. It had trouble too recouping payments due from the LNWR for the soldiers it had carried during the war on its behalf when the LNWR's ships were full. Facing financial difficulties which it could not overcome, the oldest steamship company in the world was wound up. In 1919 it sold its Dublin-Liverpool assets to the British & Irish Steam Packet Company and the following year the LNWR, which had just taken charge of new ships, was finally awarded the

This letter was one
of the very last to
be sorted on the
mail boat and
postmarked with
the H&K datestamp
for 20 February
1925. Post Office
staff were
withdrawn the
next day.
(An Post Museum
& Archive)

Post Office contract for the Kingstown-Holyhead route. On 23 November 1920 the Postmaster General, Albert Illingworth, sought the approval of the House of Commons to award the mail contract to the LNWR. Its offer of £100,000 for 20 years had, on any reasonable business examination, to be preferred to the CDSPC's tender of £150,000 for 10 years but in the old days the Irish MPs would have found a way to make a fight of it. After the 1918 election, however, Irish politics was radically changed and the old order had crumbled. Sinn Féin had won that election decisively with 73 seats and its MPs declined to go to Westminster. The Irish Parliamentary Party was reduced to 6 seats and the Irish Unionists held up well with 22 MPs. While some of these did their best for the Company, the considerable united pressure which Irish parliamentarians had been able to exert in the past on behalf of the CDSPC

was gone. There was still some interesting discussion: William Lindsay of Belfast called for an investigation of the contract by way of a Select Committee and there was genuine concern about the fate of the CDSPC's employees, most of whom would be taken on by the LNWR. There was acknowledgement that the Company's ships had been very useful during the war and an admission they had made 'very handy transport steamers'. One far-sighted MP suggested that the future of Irish mail conveyance actually lay with air transport. Jeremiah MacVeagh, MP for South Down, had no qualms about blaming the Government for the CDSPC's woes:

> *The fault is entirely due to the Government for the manner in which they treated the City of Dublin Steam Packet Company. They lost two of their steamers during the War when they were requisitioned by the Government. The Government did not pay them the compensation, but compelled them to indulge in very costly litigation, and it is the fault of the Government entirely that the City of Dublin Steam Packet Company has been placed in the position in which it finds itself to-day.* [50]

It took a few years to wind up the affairs of the CDSPC. Application for liquidation was made to the High Court of the new Irish Free State and the necessary order was granted by Mr. Justice Murnaghan in November 1924 shortly after the Company had achieved its centenary. Business was depressed and after various trade offers came to nought, the two remaining mail boats, *Ulster* and *Munster,* ended up with a German breaker. There were surplus assets and distributions were made to shareholders until 1931. The B&I line preserved the

POST-ĊEAᴚᴚTAᴚ ḃAιⱡE Áṫa CⱡιAṫ.

L.O. 21

Baile Átha Cliath, Dún Laoghaire and Holyhead Mail Service.

_____ 1945

		Proper Time A.M.	Actual Time A.M.	Causes of delay, etc.
Sorting Office	despatch	7.0	7.0	
Westland Row	dep.	7.20	7.20	
Dún Laoghaire Pier	arr.	7.33	7.34	
Last bag on board Packet		7.46	8.20	Last Pcl bag aboard 9.24 m
Packet "Cambria" started		9.20	9.30	

	No. of Bags Embarked.		
	From Early Train	From Mail Train	From Dún Laoghaire & Wexford Lines
Cross Channel	120	9	
Foreign and Colonial	102		
Parcel Post	339		

Officer in Charge of the Mails.

L & N.W. S.S. ANGLIA, LADIES DECK CABIN, HOLYHEAD & DUBLIN SERVICE.

names of two of the Provinces on its ships with the _Munster_ and the proud but tragic _Leinster_ surviving into the present generation on the Liverpool route.

The LNWR's _Hibernia, Cambria, Scotia_ and _Anglia_ were the mail boats that took over the voyage from Dún Laoghaire, as it would be called after independence, and these ships efficiently fulfilled the new Post Office contract. This provided for twenty-eight sailings per week, two a day in each direction, with parcel mails also carried by the mail boats but under a separate parcel post agreement. The original contract payment was £100,000 but the changed circumstances that came with independence saw this fall to £74,850 by 1925 and, in 1942, when the contract was extended, the figure was reduced to £65,000, of which the Irish Post Office paid

£20,000 and the British Post Office the balance. On the Holyhead & Dún Laoghaire Packet, as it had been renamed on 1 April 1922, sorting on the day service in both directions was discontinued after 10 March 1923 and Post Office staff stopped travelling on the boat altogether after the arrival of the night boat on the morning of 21 February 1925. The ships had passed into the ownership of the newly-formed London, Midland & Scottish Railway in 1923 and the _Anglia_ was subsequently withdrawn and laid up in Barrow. The _Scotia_ was sunk at Dunkirk in 1940. Service during the Second World War was reduced to one sailing a day but mail boat service remained important at that time for it carried the diplomatic pouches between London and Dublin. After the war, the two sailing standard was only partially restored, generally operating only in the

The LNWR's _Anglia_ did not serve long on the Dún Laoghaire-Holyhead route but the _Cambria_ and _Hibernia_, in their 1949 Harland & Wolff incarnation, survived until 1976. The _Cambria_'s letter bill for 10 October 1945, the anniversary of the _Leinster_'s sinking, notes a delay in getting the mails on board. (An Post Museum & Archive)

Delivering mail to the Kish Lightship in 1927. An officer of the *Scotia* throws a bag overboard to be collected by the lighthouse keeper. (Fr. FM Browne Collection/ Davisonphoto)

summer. When British Rail, the LMS's successor, sought a price increase in 1964, the two Post Offices began to assess their options in the light of competitive air-mail quotations, the introduction of roll on/roll off ferries and the move to containerisation of mail. Changed circumstances meant that the remarkable transit times that had been regularly attained on the sea and rail route until the First World War were no longer being achieved. While parcels, it was envisaged, would stay on the sea route, air-mail offered an improved service for first class letter post and when the British Post Office stopped sending first class items by sea to Ireland in the summer of 1977, it was clear that the demise of the mail boat as a vital component of Post Office operations was in sight. The ships – no longer working as mail boats but remembered locally as such by older people – continued to bring colour and life to Dún Laoghaire until Stena Line closed its passenger service in 2015 in favour of Dublin port. The last tenuous and slender thread that had once so intimately linked this once bustling seaside Victorian town with the Irish Post Office had been severed.

In this year, the centenary of the *Leinster* tragedy, it is fitting that we recall to mind packet ships and mail boats, the passengers, sailors and soldiers of every nationality who have been connected with them over the centuries, and in particular the 22 Post Office staff who were on board the RMS *Leinster* when she sailed from Kingstown on the morning of 10 October 1918.

One of the *Leinster*'s anchors was recovered in 1996 and it rests now, just a few yards from the old mail boat pier, as a permanent memorial to all those who died. (Stephen Ferguson)

Appendix 1

Post Office staff who died on the RMS *Leinster* with those dependants entitled to compensation

Post Office employee	Age	Address*	Born	Denom.	Dependants receiving compensation	Date of birth
Charles Joseph Archer	c. 31	1 Enniskerry Road, Phibsborough	Dublin	RC	Anne Elizabeth (widow) Sheila Mary Una Edward John Charles Joseph	6.8.1884 25.10.1909 5.1.1911 27.3.1914 30.6.1919
Jennins Attwooll	c. 56	15 Jones Road, Drumcondra	England	Methodist	Edith Jane (widow) William Harold Edith Doreen Mabel Hilda Charles Thrift	16.12.1872 26.1.1904 26.8.1905 11.1.1907 18.7.1909 7.11.1910
James Joseph Blake	c. 49	167 Clonliffe Road, Drumcondra	Dublin	RC	Catherine (widow) Eileen Patricia Daniel Gerard	9.12.1866 11.3.1903 8.1.1906
Thomas Joseph Bolster	c. 35	18 North Leinster Street, Phibsborough	Limerick	RC	Thomas (father) Margaret (mother)	Uncertain – over 80 Uncertain – over 80
Joseph Henry Bradley	c. 52	3 Pretoria Villas, Clontarf	Dublin	C of I	Margaret Alice (widow) Gladys Dorothy Winifred Walter	6.6.1871 12.2.1904 31.11.1909 20.6.1913 22.5.1916
Mathew Brophy	c. 35	10 Munster Street, Phibsborough	Dublin	RC	Mary (widow) Mathew Joseph Mary	28.11.1881 2.7.1914
Peter Paul Daly	c. 42	23 Richmond Road, Drumcondra	Limerick	RC	Annabel (widow) Paul Anthony Benjamin	8.9.1882 20.6.1911

*Addresses as recorded on 1911 census

Post Office employee	Age	Address*	Born	Denom.	Dependants receiving compensation	Date of birth
John Dewar	c. 36	9 Carnew Street, Stoneybatter	Scotland	Presbyterian	Agnes (widow) Mary Jean Margaret	25.1.1880 2.6.1905 14.11.1908
John Dolan	c. 39	Not found	-	-	Jane (widow) Robert Mary Patrick Anna Jacqueline Mary Eucharia	23.4.1890 17.3.1914 27.2.1915 30.5.1918
Patrick Forbes	c. 44	115 Seville Place, Dublin 1	Dublin	RC	Eliza (mother) Eliza (sister)	1851 1883
Michael Hogan	c. 42	53 North Leinster Street, Phibsborough	Laois	RC	Agnes Mary (widow) Leo Benedict Mary Agnes Kathleen Frances Michael Vincent John	26.8.1873 26.11.1909 3.6.1911 3.8.1913 14.11.1914
John Ledwidge	c. 49	1 Dalkey Avenue, Dalkey	Dublin	RC	Ellen (widow) James Leo George Joseph	21.9.1878 26.9.1903 28.3.1907
Alfred Thomas McDonnell	c. 43	7 Victoria Avenue, Donnybrook	Dublin	C of I	Elizabeth (widow) Frances Evelyn (totally incapacitated)	3.4.1868 24.5.1903 2.12.1900
William Maxwell	c. 43	57 Jones Road, Drumcondra	Fermanagh	RC	Mary Teresa (widow) Teresa William Lawrence Francis Leo Clare Kevin Annie Josephine John Jennie	16.12.1876 26.12.1903 16.11.1905 27.4.1909 6.10.1910 28.5.1912 2.1.1914 24.3.1915 14.4.1916 24.2.1918
Patrick Peter Murphy	c. 56	1 Crawford Road, Glasnevin	Dublin	RC	Mary Esther (widow)	21.4.1878

*Addresses as recorded on 1911 census

Post Office employee	Age	Address*	Born	Denom.	Dependants receiving compensation	Date of birth
William John Charles Pasker	c. 42	2 Brooklyn Terrace, Dolphin's Barn	Dublin	C of I	Kathleen (widow)	29.2.1880
					John William	27.7.1903
					George Charles	12.3.1911
Richard Patterson	c. 54	9 Leahy's Terrace, Sandymount	Dublin	C of I	Kate (widow)	30.5.1863
					Eileen	19.6.1905
Joseph Robinson	c. 42	3 Whitworth Place, Drumcondra	Galway	RC	Elizabeth Agnes	12.12.1878
					Joseph Christopher	15.10.1906
					John Francis	25.6.1909
					Elizabeth Martha	20.4.1911
					Anne Brigid	1.2.1913
					Mary Josephine	12.8.1915
					Veronica Cora	17.6.1917
Adam Smyth	c. 42	19 Sandycove Road, Dun Laoghaire	Dublin	RC	Elizabeth (widow)	- .8.1876
					John	25.10.1902
					Emily	14.11.1904
					Elizabeth	14.9.1906
					Mary Claire	10.8.1908
					Gertrude Frances	26.11.1910
					Eileen	13.9.1912
					Adam	2.2.1914
					James	2.10.1916
William Henry Wakefield	c. 35	84 Lower Drumcondra Road	Longford	RC	Agnes (widow)	24.8.1891
					Charles Henry	28.10.1912
					William Frederick	31.5.1914
					Louisa Mary	12.9.1915
					Agnes Teresa	17.12.1917
James Alfred Warbrook	c. 51	2 Wolseley Street, Dolphin's Barn	Offaly	C of I	Annie (widow)	19.7.1867

*Addresses as recorded on 1911 census

Endnotes

1   A piece of the *Leinster's* deck also acts as a memorial in Holyhead.

2   B. Cunningham, *Calendar of State Papers relating to Ireland 1568-1571* (Revised edition) (Dublin: Irish Manuscripts Commission, 2010) p. 143.

3   C. W. Russell & J. P. Prendergast (eds.), *Calendar of the State Papers relating to Ireland 1606-1608* (London: Longmans…etc., 1874) p. 454.

4   R. P. Mahaffy (ed.) *Calendar of State Papers relating to Ireland 1669-1670*, (London: HMSO, 1910) p. 114.

5   *Report from Select Committee on Holyhead Roads* (London: House of Commons, 1815) p. 5.

6   *Report from the Select Committee on Communication between London and Dublin* (London: House of Commons, 1853) p. iv.

7   *Twenty-second Report of the Commissioners of Inquiry into the Collection and Management of the Revenue arising in Ireland and Great Britain. Post-Office Revenue, United Kingdom: Part V. Packet Establishments – Home Stations.* (London: House of Commons, 1830) p. 31.

8   On 3 July 1905 a supplementary night mail service was introduced to Ireland. A 10.15 p.m. dispatch from Euston met an LNWR boat at Holyhead at 3.55 a.m. This docked at the North Wall and letters were delivered in Dublin between 9 a.m. and 10 a.m.. The LNWR also operated a Holyhead-North Wall Saturday service at this period specifically to accelerate outward American mails via the Cunard ships that called at Queenstown.

9   *Select Committee on Communication, op. cit.,* p. v.

10 *Seventh Report of the Postmaster General on the Post Office* (London: HMSO, 1861) p. 7.

11 The Postal Museum Post 12/10

12 *The Irish Mails Question* (Dublin, Council of the Chamber of Commerce, 1894) pp. 35,54

13 The Postal Museum Post 31/3a part 2.

14 *Forty-third Report of the Postmaster General on the Post Office* (London: HMSO, 1897) p. 6.

15 Ibid.

16 *Select Committee on Communication, op. cit.,* p. 15.

17 Ibid. p. 133.

18 Ibid. p. 90.

19 After 1916, the sorting office was moved to a temporary premises behind the Rotunda hospital and later to a new office in Pearse Street. It never returned to the GPO.

20 E. J. Hart, '*With Her Majesty's Mails to Ireland*' in *The Strand Magazine* (London, George Newnes, 1895) p.410.

21 Wirral Archives Service, 005/0279/010. The *Leinster's* specification drawings are not currently accessible but some were reproduced by Roy Stokes in his *Death in the Irish Sea.*

22 The Postal Museum Post 31/3a part 2.

23 M. Sefi, 'The Transatlantic Post Office 1905-1914' in *The London Philatelist* Vol. 127 No. 1453, p. 69.

24 The Postal Museum Post 31/2b.

25 Ibid.

26 E. Watson, *The Royal Mail to Ireland* (London: Edward Arnold, 1917) p. 236.

27 Laird's trial book, ZCL4/5/406, in the collection of Wirral Archives Service records their speeds as only slightly slower than the destroyers their yards also built. The destroyers, however, were considerably shorter and lighter than the mail boats.

28 The Postal Museum Post 31/92c.

29 The *Irish Times* 11 October 1918, quoting Mr. W. Gaynor of Ballylusky, Nenagh.

30 NLI, Ms 2885 Journal of the *Ulster* 1918.

31 R. Stokes, *Death in the Irish Sea,* (Cork, The Collins Press, 1998) p. 55.

32 The Postal Museum Post 31/92c

33 It is possible that Higgins made a mistake in identifying Attwooll as the man to whom he spoke for on a later occasion he identified that colleague as Pat Murphy.

34 The Postal Museum Post 31/92c.

35 Ibid.

36 Ibid.

37 *The Irish Postal & Telegraph Guardian* Vol. 14 No. 9 p. 5.

38 The *Times* 12 October 1918.

39 The *Irish Times*, 17 October 1918, quoting James MacMahon, Under Secretary.

40 *Hansard* House of Commons debates, 17 October 1918.

41 *Hansard* House of Lords debates, 22 October 1918.

42 Ibid.

43 Ibid. 23 October 1918.

44 PRONI D627/434/80 Letter from Hugh Barrie, Coleraine, Co. Londonderry, to Hugh de Fellenberg Montgomery, Fivemiletown, Co. Tyrone.

45 *Hansard* House of Commons debates 15 October 1916.

46 The Postal Museum Post 31/92c.

47 *Hansard* House of Commons debates 14 July 1918.

48 The *Freeman's Journal* 29 October 1918.

49 P. Lecane, *Torpedoed* (Penzance, Periscope Publishing Ltd., 2005) p. 279.

50 *Hansard* House of Commons debates 23 December 1920,

Acknowledgements

I am grateful to all those who have assisted me with the work for this book, colleagues in An Post, staff at The Postal Museum in London, Wirral Archives Services, the National Library of Ireland, Trinity College Dublin, the Irish Labour History Museum, the National Maritime Museum and elsewhere. Permission to reproduce photographs of items in their possession is much appreciated, as is David Davison's help in finding some lovely photographs of mail boats, and if any misattribution of ownership has occurred, please make it known to the publisher so that it can be noted and corrected in any future edition of the book. My wife's encouragement and practical help was, as always, invaluable.

Select Bibliography

Primary sources

Report from the Select Committee on Holyhead Roads (London: House of Commons, 1815)

Twenty-second Report of the Commissioners of Inquiry into the Collection and Management of the Revenue arising in Ireland and Great Britain. Post-Office Revenue, United Kingdom: Part V. Packet Establishments – Home Stations. (London: House of Commons, 1830)

First report of the Committee appointed by the Lords of the Treasury … relative to the best means of communicating between London and Dublin and the relative Capabilities of the ports of Holyhead, Ormes bay, and Portdynallaen, (London: House of Commons, 1840)

Report from the Select Committee on Post Office Communication with Ireland (London: House of Commons, 1842)

Report from the Select Committee on Communication between London and Dublin 1853 (London: House of Commons, 1853)

Report of the Committee appointed by the Treasury to enquire into the Acceleration of the Irish Day Mails (London: HMSO, 1898)

Post Office (Contract for Accelerated Mail Service to and from Ireland via Carlisle, Stranraer and Larne) (London: HMSO, 1903)

Correspondence relating to the Arrangement made in 1898 for the Acceleration of the Irish Day Mail Service, and the revision of the same in the present year (London: HMSO, 1908)

American Mail Service – Omission of Call at Queenstown by Cunard Packets (London: HMSO 1914)

Reports of the Postmaster General on the Post Office (London: HMSO, 1855-1922)

Cunningham, B., *Calendar of State Papers relating to Ireland 1568-1571* (Dublin: Irish Manuscripts Commission 2010)

Russell, C W & Prendergast J P, *Calendar of State Papers relating to Ireland 1606-1608* (London: Longmans…etc 1874)

Secondary sources

- *The Story of the Irish Mail (London: London Midland and Scottish Railway, nd)*
- *Dublin and Holyhead & Kingstown Packet P.O. Circulation List (Dublin: HMSO, 1909)*
- *The Irish Mails Question (Dublin: Council of the Chamber of Commerce, 1894)*

Ayres, G., *History of the Mail Routes to Ireland until 1850* (Np,lulu.com, 2011)

de Courcy Ireland, J., *History of Dun Laoghaire Harbour* (Dublin: Edward Burke, 2001)

Daunton, M. J., *Royal Mail - The Post Office since 1840* (London: Athlone Press, 1985)

Elis-Williams, M., *Packet to Ireland* (Caernarfon: Gwynedd Archives Service, 1984)

Ferguson, S., *The Post Office in Ireland - An Illustrated History* (Newbridge: Irish Academic Press, 2016)

Hart, E. J., 'With Her Majesty's Mails to Ireland', *The Strand Magazine* (London, George Newnes, 1895)

Hendy, J. G., *Historical Summary of Mail Communications between Great Britain and Ireland* (Unpublished typescript at The Postal Museum Post12/10)

Hitches, M., *The Irish Mail* (Stroud: Sutton Publishing Limited, 2000)

Hosking, R., *The Transatlantic Post Office*, (Oxted: Roger Hosking, 1979)

Kidd, C., *The Irish Mail* (London: Robson Lowe Limited, nd)

Leathem, J. G., 'Observations on the present method of contracting for the Mail Packet Service', *Journal of the Dublin Statistical Society* Part XV, January 1860 (Dublin: McGlashan and Gill, 1860)

Lecane, P., *Torpedoed* (Penzance: Periscope Publishing Ltd., 2005)

Lovelock, A. D., *Postal markings of the Holyhead & Kingstown Packet 1860-1925* (The TPO & Seapost Society, 2006)

McDonnell, A., 'Adam Smyth (1875-1918) Post Office Sorter on Royal Mail Steamer "Leinster"', *Journal of the Genealogical Society of Ireland* Vol. 5 No. 1 (Dublin: 2004)

Norway, A. H., *History of the Post-Office Packet Service* (London: Macmillan, 1896)

Robinson, H., *The British Post Office – A History* (Princeton, NJ: Princeton University Press, 1948)

Salt, D., *The Domestic Packets between Great Britain and Ireland, 1635 to 1840* (London: the Postal History Society, 1991)

Sefi, M., 'The Transatlantic Post Office 1905-1914', *The London Philatelist* Vol. 127 No. 1453 (London: The Royal Philatelic Society, 2018)

Stokes, R., *Death in the Irish Sea* (Cork: The Collins Press, 1998)

Tutty, M. J., 'The City of Dublin Steam Packet Company', *Dublin Historical Record* Vol. XVIII (Dublin: Old Dublin Society, 1963)

Yeates, A. C., '70 years of the Irish Mail', *Sea Breezes*, Vol. 32 (Liverpool: Charles Birchall & Sons, 1961)

Watson, E., *The Royal Mail to Ireland* (London: Edward Arnold, 1917)

Index

An enlarged detail of a formal photograph of the Dublin Post Office men who worked on the mail boats. Taken in 1910 some of these men would lose their lives on the *Leinster*. (An Post Museum & Archive)

Irish Mail.

Sackville Street, Dublin.

H&K. P&CT
OC 3
5
1918

SALVED FROM
S.S. "LEINSTER".

Aston and Mander Ltd

Albany Works

Tr...

THREE HALFPENCE

Recovered from RMS Leinster

THREE HALFPENCE

Vesey C.B.G.
R.B.M.C.
...attside
Finchley Rd.
London
N.W. 2.

CARTWELL & MC.DONALD
DUBLIN.

DUBLIN
OCT 9
5.30 PM
1918

DAMAGED BY IMMERSION
IN SEA WATER. L.8

Messrs. Grant, Hughes & Co.,
21, Mincing Lane
LONDON E.C. 3

Published by
An Post
General Post Office
Lower O'Connell Street
Dublin 1

© Stephen Ferguson 2018

ISBN: 9781872228730

Design: Vermillion
Index: Kate Murphy
Print: Castuera

Playing Outside
Activities, Ideas and Inspiration for the Early Years

Helen Bilton

This edition reprinted 2009 by Routledge
2 Park Square, Milton Park, Abingdon, Oxon, OX14 4RN
Simultaneously published in the USA and Canada by Routledge
270 Madison Avenue, New York, NY 10016

Reprinted 2004, 2005, 2006, 2008, 2009

10 9 8 7 6

British Library Cataloguing in Publication Data
A catalogue recort for this book is available from the British
Library.

ISBN 1 84312 067 4

Typeset by Matrix Creative, Wokingham
Printed and bound in Great Britain

Contents

Acknowledgements

Heartfelt thanks go to the following people and settings. This book could not have been written without you.

Sasha from **Jack and Jill's Playgroup**, King's Lynn.

Southmead Primary School, Wandsworth, particularly Beth, Rosie and Shona.

Balham Nursery School, Wandsworth, particularly May, Claire and Helen.

Strathmore Infant and Nursery School, Hertfordshire, particularly Lucky and Carol.

Coombes Nursery and Infant School, Wokingham, particularly Sue, Anne and Donna.

Caversham Nursery School, Caversham.

Ambleside Centre, Woodley.

Wimbledon Jewish Nursery School, Wandsworth, particularly Judith.

Rob Nicholson, Head of Early Years, **Wandsworth Borough Council**.

Sarah MacCraiger, Senior Early Years Development Officer, **Wandsworth Borough Council**.

Sue Kronda, Adviser for Assessment, **Hertfordshire County Council**.

Diane Croston, Adviser for Assessment, **Hertfordshire County Council**.

Karen Musgrove, Curriculum Development Adviser for Foundation Stage and Key Stage 1, **Essex County Council**.

Aboyne Lodge, Hertfordshire.

Four Swannes Primary School, Hertfordshire.

Goldfield Infant School, Hertfordshire.

St John's JMI School, Hertfordshire.

Norcot Nursery School, Reading.

Victoria Park Nursery School, West Berkshire.

Baylis Court Nursery School, Slough.

Judith Thompson, Pre-school Worker, **Traveller Education Service**, Gloucester.

Introduction – setting the scene

This book attempts to bring outdoor play alive through images of children playing outside. In my travels over the last couple of years I have been able to talk to practitioners in the early years field and to find out how they are managing to run outdoor play successfully. Also I have been able to discuss possible changes and then follow this up with how the changes have impacted on practice.

The book is divided into five chapters. Each chapter discusses the issues and provides ideas, photos, case studies and questions to ask. The first chapter looks at the various reasons for having outdoor play and how playing outside can impact favourably on children. Chapter 2 looks at what the adult needs to be doing to make playing outside for children successful. The third chapter explains how to offer the whole curriculum outside, sharing ideas from a range of settings. It includes resource lists, ideas and issues to think about for each bay. Chapter 4 discusses those issues which can make or break outdoor play, namely resources, bikes, the weather, fixed equipment, in and out available simultaneously, combining activities in and out and the layout. Finally, Chapter 5 discusses a project to change outdoor play in reception and nursery classes, how a unit runs outdoor play and weather boxes. It looks to the future and how playing outside is good for children of all ages. At the end of the book the Resources and contacts section provides details of useful books and activity packs, suppliers of equipment and where to obtain advice.

Introduction –
setting the scene

Chapter 1
Do we need outdoor play?

Any educational experience is made of the who, the what and the how, that is:

the children (who) the curriculum or knowledge (what) and the environment (how)

We have to be convinced that children will gain from an educational experience so in this chapter I will be putting the case for providing outdoor play. How we bring the children and knowledge together is crucial in making the educational experience worthwhile. Done badly, outdoor play does little for any child; done well, outdoor play can help and support children as they think, feel and act.

Figure 1.1a *Children active, absorbed and purposeful*

Figure 1.1b Children active, absorbed and purposeful

The play shown in Figure 1.1 a–e went on for an hour; two children were continuously involved while many others went in and out of the play. The scene was a cat stuck up a tree and most of the play and discussion was around how to rescue this cat.

Resources included ropes, material, a half-metre diameter cable spool, pegs, pens, chalks, paper and an adult. The adult was called when the children needed her and she collaborated in the problem-solving exercise (Anne is not cross but problem solving wuth the children!). Skills included estimation, fixing, placing, negotiation, co-operation, writing and planning. This was a worthwhile educational experience, because the children learned so much.

Figure 1.1c, d, e Children active, absorbed and purposeful

Figure 1.2 Seven fire fighters working together and using vacuum cleaner hoses as water hoses

Three reasons for having outdoor play

Reason 1

Outside is a natural environment for children; there is a freedom associated with the space that cannot be replicated inside.

Case study

William, aged nine said:

'Sometimes I feel really itchy and spikey when I get home from school and not very nice, but if I go outside then I feel okay again and I am not horrible to anyone.'

This child knows how he feels in different environments and how that then impacts on people around him.

If children feel at home in a particular space it seems logical to teach them in that area; education should not be a chore but an enjoyable and worthwhile occupation. Ask any grown up about their childhood and a glazed expression will come over them when they talk about going outside to play! They talk in terms of doing their own thing, staying away from grown ups, spending lots of time with friends, negotiating and co-operating to make things, having and sorting out arguments, having fun, getting really worn out and just simply relaxing. Outdoors is somewhere most children like to be, but it needs to be enjoyable, fun, relaxing and involve others (see Figure 1.2). The grown ups mention learning in terms of learning about being with other people and learning how to give and take, understand and forgive. Grown ups don't often mention the formal curriculum, but they will have learnt about every subject area of life.

Reason 2

The environment in which children and adults play and work affects emotions, behaviour, personality and the ability to learn. The environment can affect different children differently.

* Some children prefer to work and play outside. Certain children seem to prefer to play inside, some outside and some seem able to utilise both areas. Often it seems that many boys prefer to play outside. However, even those children who prefer to play outside, given good inside and outside areas, will utilise both but the inside area to a lesser extent. At the 2003 Institute of Education Early Years Conference in London one of the delegates pointed out that traveller children and often refugee children prefer to be outside, as this is where they naturally live for most of the day. For them they *need* to be outside as this is where they feel empowered.

* Some children are less inhibited outside. You can find in a setting one child with two personalities, one associated with inside and one outside. Inside a child can be reticent, shy, unwilling to get involved with many of the activities. However, outside the same child can be vocal, effervescent and perfectly happy to have a go at any activity. It would appear that the affecting force is walls and a ceiling; this is sufficient to affect the child's whole personality.

Figure 1.3 A cold day, but still wanting to read outside

* Some children are more able outside. Outside play for some children can involve more mature discussions, more advanced play and more ability. For me the very crucial issue is that if these children are tested/judged/assessed outside they would be found to be more able than if they were judged inside.

* Some children are more assertive and imaginative outside. Being assertive means being able to put one's ideas or point of view forward, and being confident enough to take a lead role in the play, this can only occur for certain children if they are playing in an outdoor area.

* Some children will use activities placed outside which they would not use inside. Boys can feel reticent about books and writing and for some there is a greater risk to putting pen to paper than climbing a ten-metre fence. When books are placed in an environment that children feel secure in they are able to access them (see Figure 1.3). For others it may be painting, or building and construction. Older children tend to prefer to play imaginatively outside and will not access this type of resource inside.

* Some children can concentrate and persevere for longer outside. Boys' activity span can be longer outside than inside and longer than girls' span outside. It would appear that adults differ in where they can concentrate: some need total quiet, others seem to cope with interruption, and likewise children are different in their tolerance levels. To concentrate we need to be interested in the activity, happy with the space we are working in and aware that mistakes are okay. For some children this type of atmosphere is only prevalent outside.

* Some children will learn more outside than inside. It would seem to follow that if children feel able, secure and confident they are likely to learn more than if they are feeling unable, insecure and lacking in confidence.

Reason 3

Outdoors is a perfect place to learn through movement, one of the four vehicles through which children can learn, the others being play, talk and sensory experience. However, for learning through movement to truly work there needs to be enough space to move, do and find out. In overcrowded spaces children's behaviour can change, causing aggressive and gang like behaviour in the boys and solitary behaviour in the girls (Dates 1986). Learning by doing may involve pulling a truck, digging or arranging blocks in a particular space. All of these activities need enough space to be worthwhile. Through activities such as these children will not only learn and find out many concepts and learning attitudes but they will also benefit from becoming healthy and staying so. It is so very important for children to be vigorous in their movements, to the extent that the heart and lungs are working hard, and they get out of breath. The activity needs to be daily and simply part of the routine of the day; children who experience activity as part of their day, tend to go on to adulthood in the same vein. Exercise can also affect emotions, allowing for relaxation and calmness and a heightened sense of well-being (Armstrong 1996). Sports England is running a scheme to encourage schools to keep children active, fit and healthy. The Qualifications and Curriculum Authority reports that pupils achieved higher grades and were better behaved in schools where sport is taken seriously: 'It said schools that have invested in physical education and sport have seen remarkable improvements in everything from attendance and behaviour to attainment and attitudes to learning' (Curtis 2003).

Figure 1.5 Running to catch the dragons

Figure 1.4 Jumping from a height

Case study

Sulmah was a shy and reticent child when she started nursery at age three. Her first language was Urdu and she was working in English outside the home and community. She stayed with one particular member of staff for the first few weeks at nursery, and would only go outside if this staff member was with her. She tended to wander and watch but not partake of activities, even though the staff member tried to encourage her. One day a huge colony of wood lice and one stag beetle were discovered in the minibeast area. This seemed to be the catalyst for Sulmah, she was absolutely fascinated by this discovery and stayed watching them for around half an hour, leading on to drawing a variety of the insects. The next day Sulmah strode outside without the staff member to watch the insects in the minibeast area. This was followed by a strong desire to communicate verbally with staff members about the happenings in the minibeast area and her confidence from that day grew and grew. Through this experience it seems Sulmah found the confidence to communicate and act; she may have had an experience inside which would have created the same spark, but she may not. This outdoor experience affected Sulmah emotionally and linguistically and therefore intellectually.

Conclusion

So, yes, we do need outdoor play, so that all children can work in an environment they feel secure in, whatever the activity. Children in a good outdoor play area will appear active, absorbed, motivated and purposeful – a very satisfying sight (see Figure 1.1).

Questions

What do children say about the outdoor area?

Have you noticed any differences in the children's behaviour, personality or actions outside in comparison to inside?

Does outdoor provision reflect what is going on in the children's lives?

Do you assess children outside?

How often do the children get out of breath? (See Figures 1.4–1.7).

Figure 1.6 Skipping

Figure 1.7 Pushing and pulling the removals truck

Chapter 2
The adult's role before, during and after outdoor play

Children need freedom outside but they do not need a free for all; it is the adult's job to make sure all children can learn, enjoy and reach their potential. You 'reap what you sow': if outside consists of a few bikes, a climbing frame and uninterested adults then it is likely that the children will argue about the few toys, not learn very much and feel dissatisfied when they go inside; if you provide quality outdoor play, children will become confident, independent and learn a great deal.

Figure 2.1 Children and adult playing together. The children were taking the lead.

Siraj-Blatchford and Sylva, researching the effective pedagogy in the early years, found that children do well in terms of:

cognitive development in settings ... where there was a good balance between child and adult-initiated activities, and where well-qualified staff were skilled in 'extending' or developing the children's activities. Free play was on the menu, but so were more focused group activities.

(Northen 2003: 15)

Type of demand	Number of demands in 20 minutes
To play	
To have a conversation	
To ask for help	
To show something	
To ask a question to do with learning	
To explain something	
To find resources	
To fix something	
To sort out a disagreement	
To ask permission – e.g. toilet	

Key

Play – when a child specifically asks an adult to play with them

Conversation – when a child simply comes for a chat often about their life, what they have been doing, going to do

Help – when a child is making something and needs an adult's help. This is very often to hold something

Show – when a child needs to celebrate a product or process

Question – where a child is involved in learning and requires an answer, 'Why has that changed colour?', 'Why is the water moving?', 'Why won't these stay in?'

Explain – to show why something has happened, regarding what they are doing now or have found out in the past

Find – where an adult is needed to collect resources which a child cannot reach, or is not allowed to take

Fix – to mend something which has come apart or broken

Disagreement – where children are in disagreement and need adult assistance whether it be over a resource or toy, but not about a fact

Permission – where children are expected to ask to go to the toilet, to collect coats, change activity

Figure 2.2 Children's and adults' interacting demands, adapted from Dunne and Bennett's (2003) observation schedule

Staff with a positive attitude

Staff need to be supportive towards outdoor play! If the whole staff group want to use outside effectively this is half the battle, but this is not always the case. One way of getting staff on board is to look objectively at what is happening outside and to identify the problem areas.

The play pro formas (Figures 2.2–2.4) can help with this, and it is quite simple to devise one's own.

Sometimes staff simply do not understand outdoor play or how children actually learn outside.

Case study

Lucky decided to involve the whole staff group in looking at how children were playing in their nursery /reception unit, using a plan of the garden area to mark where children played over the whole session. This highlighted areas that were being used well or not, areas staff frequented and not and what specific children preferred to do and not do. As a consequence Lucky decided to cross-reference the learning outcomes from the *Curriculum Guidance for the Foundation Stage* (QCA 2000) and what activities could demonstrate this (see Figure 2.5). This helped staff identify the potential and learning possibilities of the activities.

Activity	Name of child:					
↕	↦					

In the left-hand column note all activities within the setting (you may need more boxes). Every five minutes note who is playing where, the row boxes denoting five-minute intervals.

Figure 2.3 Child activity involvement

Planning

Outside is a half of a whole, inside being the other half. If the two environments are viewed together then the planning needs to be viewed as such. Nicholson (2003) suggests incorporating outdoors in the plans for indoors, so only one document is needed, outside activities complementing indoors and vice versa. Some planning simply lists resources, with no indication of learning possibilities, skills or attitudes to be taught. However, it is more effective to note down what it is you are trying to achieve with the children, the actual activities to be carried out and questions to be asked, as in Figure 2.6a, an example of medium-term planning, and Figure 2.6b, an example of short-term planning.

There are many ways to plan; the case studies offered here are not given as definitive, but to provide ideas. It is impossible to actually demonstrate the amount of discussion that will go on before and after the planning, but for planning to work there has to be a reasonable amount of time devoted to discussions. This is demonstrated by the example provided in Figure 2.7, planning for activities outside and in. Note the many links made to inside activities and the comments from past learning and future plans.

Case study

Southmead Primary School (see also p. 90) has a nursery/reception unit, comprising 81 children per session, aged three to five, with a staff group of 3 teachers, 3 nursery nurses and 5 assistants. The unit is organised into five areas of development (physical; mathematical; communication, language and literacy; knowledge and understanding; and creative) and this is reflected in five separate planning sheets each week, each sheet having a particular focus but covering all the areas of learning. An example of one of these sheets is shown in Figure 2.8. Personal, social and emotional development is expected to happen everywhere. So for example the outdoors is classed as the physical area, and the planning will give a movement focus but then offer activities for all areas

Activity	Location of adult						
↕	⟶						

List activities in the left-hand column, including incidentals such as clearing up, taking child to toilet and so on, (you may need more boxes). Note every five minutes where the adult is, each row denoting a five-minute interval, or note the activity the adult is involved with, every time they move.

Figure 2.4 Adult activity involvement

of the curriculum. One of the reasons for planning in this way is to ensure those children who stay in one area, often new children, can access the whole curriculum through the one learning area. One focused activity is offered inside and one outside each day.

Each evening the staff discuss how the day has gone and in the light of the findings plan for the next day. Every Thursday, staff consider all areas and plan for the following week. Figure 2.9 is an example of the activity and child evaluation.

Stepping Stones/Early Learning Goals	Outdoor activities
Mathematical Development	
* Say and use number names in order in familiar contexts	Throwing balls into tyres, at hanging bottles, through hanging hoops – keeping score; writing numbers on the blackboard; imaginative role play – phoning for an ambulance/police/fire engine
* Reliably count up to ten everyday objects	Counting the balls/tyres/hoops/hats/cars/prams/other resources when tidying up; looking for minibeasts/leaves/conkers/stones/twigs etc. and counting the amount found; counting how many bricks children have used to make a small/tall tower
* Recognise numerals 1 – 9	Matching number tiles to the number ladder; number hunts; parking cars in numbered parking spaces; throwing balls at numbers written on the wall/ground; reading number plates, house numbers; making parking tickets; finding hidden numbers in the sand, coloured water, paint in shallow trays
* Use own methods to solve a problem	Transporting bricks/crates/boxes – finding how many will balance on the trolley; estimating how many conkers/stones will fit into different containers – why some will hold more/less
* Begin to use mathematical names for 'solid' 3D shapes and 'flat' 2D shapes and mathematical terms to describe shapes	Shape hunt, building with large blocks – using vocabulary, e.g. 'I need a flat/square/pointy one' when making houses, towers, bridges etc.; painting shapes on the ground; painting parts of the playhouse and talking about the shape of the door, windows and roof; making shapes – squirting

Figure 2.5 Cross-referencing the learning outcomes to outdoor activities

Medium-term planning

Start date:

Expected end date:

Theme: Minibeasts

Personal, social and emotional development

Broad learning intentions

To understand the need to care for living things
To show interest and involvement
To persist in looking for living things
To collaborate and share learning with others
To look to others for support in learning

Key activities and starting points

Set up a minibeast environment outside
Set up an inside minibeast area, having observed outside
Encouraging children to share knowledge and observations
Paired activities – one observes and the other draws
Set up a science resource base
Read *The Bad Tempered Ladybird*

Communication, language and literacy

Broad learning intentions

To use increasingly descriptive spoken language
To talk to others about what has been observed
To record observations with pictures and writing
To use resource book, tapes, video and CD-ROM to access background information
To learn and devise rhymes, poems and songs about small creatures

Key activities and starting points

Resource display of books etc.
Dictaphone tape recordings
Children preparing talks on what they have seen
Using insect big book outside and to support talks
Provide minibeast key word cards in writing area
Set up role-play animal hospital

Creative development

Broad learning intentions

To observe and respond to minibeasts through movement, art and craft, music and play
To express and communicate a wide range of outdoor experiences

Key activities and starting points

Make minibeast puppets and develop a series of shows
Make and provide dressing-up clothes: ladybird, spider, butterfly
Make a collection of instruments for minibeast music
Sing 'caterpillars only crawl'
Use wire and moulding materials for minibeast sculpture

Physical development

Broad learning intentions

To use scientific equipment with care and control
To handle a wide range of small apparatus
To give thought to whole-body movements
To develop the confidence to climb and crawl
To be aware of hygiene when in contact with minibeasts and their environment

Key activities and starting points

Provide tweezers, droppers, nets and teach correct ways of using
Extend the outdoor small equipment range – add small balls and bats
Use play frame imaginatively to move in response to insect observations

Mathematics

Broad learning intentions

To count in a variety of contexts
To calculate with numbers with which children are confident
To look at shapes in the natural world and recreate
To investigate measuring of length

Key activities and starting points

Counting and tallying numbers of insects in log pile
Measure worms!
Making plasticine worms of particular lengths
Using magnifiers to find and describe shapes in creatures
Minibeast calculating games [home-made]

Knowledge & understanding of the world

Broad learning intentions

To make observations and record verbally
To make observations and record with pictures and models
To make suggestions based on observations
To recognise some of the conditions some creatures prefer
To use CD-ROMS to find extra information
To select a range of resources independently

Key activities and starting points

Set up a range of environments outside and inside
Provide a bank of books and CDs
Make a collection of sound recordings of our observations
Visit to retillary at Syon Park to see creatures from other places in the world

Figure 2.6a Example of medium-term planning (Source: from Nicholson 2001)

Short-term planning

Week beginning:

Learning intentions	Activities, experience and language	Resources	Links	Children	Comments
What do we want children to learn?	What do you want children to do?	We need:			What have they learnt? what next?
To show interest, involvement and perseverance	Look at log pile with small groups and magnifiers. Provide small pots and bug viewers	Log pile Pots Viewers Collection of magnifiers	K & U	Rahena Rubina Tommy Jody Mustafizur	
To know that we need to take care of living things	Provide clipboards and paper close to log pile Adults to lead investigations talking about the need to be careful and gentle				
To be able to talk about what is seen at the time and later	Children to talk informally about their observations and thoughts with other children on the mat	'Insect Body Parts' book	K & U	More confident speakers	
To use descriptive language	Introduce 'Insect Body Parts' big book – focus on magnified pictures	Clay Plasticine Playdough Fabric Cord String Paper strip roll			
To listen to others and ask questions about what they say	Adult supported drawing and writing in writing area				
To record observations with adult support	Use clay, plasticine and playdough on different days to make model of what has been seen			All children but in two small groups	
To use language, e.g. longer, shorter, the same, when making comparisons	Make worms of various lengths and play games guessing which is the longest and shortest				
To recognise that long things are not always straight	Count the insects collected in pots, at the log heap – who has the most, least? etc.	Photographs of creatures that have been enlarged	C D	All children Group 1 and 2 Group 3 and 4	
To count objects that cannot be moved	Provide various magnifiers inside with various things to look at – including text and pictures		K & U		
To make observations using magnifiers and viewers	Set up instrument collection, e.g. scrapers, twisters and tuned percussion, to respond freely to observations of minibeasts through music			Nusrath Joshua Milo	
To understand magnifiers make things appear larger					
To handle magnifiers appropriately					Available to all children – support less confident

Figure 2.6b Example of short-term planning (Source: from Nicholson 2001)

Evaluation and planning forecast

The previous fortnight has been rather unsettled for a number of reasons. This means that this current fortnight we have to revisit some Early Learning Goals and activities while developing others.

Fortnight beginning: 10 March

Cognitive and skills	Early Learning Goals	Suggested activities
Language and literacy *Book making developing — adult as scribe popular. The Maisie story prop also popular. Some children continue to find social communication difficult.*	* *continue with focus on enhancing social/communication through language (see theme)* * *develop theme work on retelling stories*	* *see personal and social/moral and spiritual link* * *link to imaginative play (domestic play/male dolls/hospital in Back class)* * *use new story tapes* * *book making (digital camera/adult as scribe)*
Mathematics *Toy collection introduced — needs developing as does spoon collection. Shape work as ongoing activities — needs more developing. Children starting to sort by size.*	* *use toy and spoon collections for sorting/matching/counting etc.* * *introduction and developing understanding of time* * *developing shape — see theme* * *matching/sorting/ordering*	* *toy and spoon collections — link with K & U* * *Use of sandtimers, stopwatches, sequencing — link with physical* * *shape/pattern/tesselation/symmetry* * *using everyday objects/children*
K & U of the world (Science) *Lots of interest in changes in the garden (growth) and the warmer weather. Children looking for birds and listening to bird song. Continue to look for patterns in the garden.*	*Theme work* * *observing/discussing changes in seasons* * *use of toy and spoon collections to develop interest linked to other areas*	* *record changes in drawings and paintings and use a camera* * *use of magnifying glasses* * *materials, history, geography, cultures — old/new discussions* * *matching games for pattern matching*
K & U of the world (Human & social) *Back class children still to go on tours of school. Spoon and toy collections to be developed. Walks looking at local environment started and very informative.*	* *explore and feel secure immediate school environment* * *explore local environment to support mosaic work (link SEN and EAL)*	* *tours of the school building and meeting all staff. Explore secret garden* * *walks around local environment looking at patterns, colours, shapes etc.*
K & U of the world (Technology) *Two simple programs used for developing children's different levels of understanding and use of mouse and keyboard skills. TINY MOUSE is good. Digital camera not used by children for books or mosaic work.*	* *continue to develop children's understanding and use of computers and programs* * *to develop children's skills when using digital camera*	* *use of two simple programs and PIXIES in both classes* * *use of other programs* * *use of digital camera by children to make books, record work and record mosaic work (preparation and actual)*
Creative and aesthetic *Use of Action Man/Barbie type dolls popular with some children. 'Helicopter' stories working well in Back class, not yet in Front class. Continue to link imaginative play in all areas.*	* *to develop imaginative play through familiar toys (link SEN and EAL)* * *link to making own stories and acting them out*	* *continue to use Action Man/Barbie type dolls in different areas* * *possible use of above dolls to facilitate for some children* * *link to play in various areas* * *musical activities and music continue*
Personal and social/moral and spiritual *Above dolls encouraged concentration and collaborative play. Many children have been unsettled due to disrupted second week plus staff on courses.*	* *continue to develop to encourage relationships (positive) with children (link SEN and EAL)* * *support all children to resettle into routines (self-confidence)*	* *links to all areas of provision* * *circle time — using related scenarios* * *saying nice things* * *use of feeling dolls* * *reassurance by staff and routines again*
Physical *Lots of interest in digging, also looking for worms. Some children using 'push' toys daily — real interest. Some children very adventurous with climbing frame equipment. Good co-operative work when moving/adjusting equipment for gradient work.*	* *continue to develop co-ordination, balancing, jumping, steering, push/pull* * *continue co-operative physical work*	* *balancing objects on head, arms etc.* * *moving along circuits — straight lines/wavy lines* * *use of push/pull vehicles — link imaginative* * *building, designing with construction and large pieces of equipment*

Figure 2.7 Planning for activities outside and in at Balham Nursery School

Social/Emotional/Attitude

Again there has been a tone of unsettled behaviour and routines. Children not all settled into routines after half term. The idea from Beata's course has worked very well for helping some children settle and focus, plus initiate communication with others. Continue this work with specific children.

SEN and EAL

D: to be involved regularly in circle times (three children + D). Children to say something nice about each child.

A: encourage use of climbing frame to develop his gross motor movements and spatial awareness. Encourage him to walk slowly.

V: ensure she is included in EAL and focus activities.

F: sing instructions/comments to him.

I: introduce a Makaton word(s) per week to all children to help I and children to communicate.

Focus children	Focused observations
1. Kriss	1. Olive
2. Angela	2. Sarah
3. James	3. Tyrell
4. Hayley	4. Michael
5. Jonathan	5. Norma
6. Lisa	6. Abby

Focus children	Focused observations
1. Olive	1. Kelsey
2. Sarah	2. Sharon
3. Tyrell	3. Jermaine
4. Michael	4. Kaldeep
5. Norma	5. Dusty
6. Abby	6. Darren

Visits and outings

Event: *Red Nose Day 14 March*

Parental Involvement: *Playing with books course. Parents (cleared) to be encouraged to work in school via rotas and encouragement of staff.*

Area plan for week beginning 7/4/03
Green/Brown (Adults responsible Donna and Beth)

	Personal, social and emotional development	Communication, language and literacy development	Mathematical development	Knowledge and understanding of the world	Physical development	Creative development
Easter egg hunt – for clues use positional language and involve shapes	Show confidence and the ability to stand up for their rights	Link sound to letters, naming and sounding letters of the alphabet	Find items from positional/directional clues / Observe and use positional language / Use shapes appropriately for tasks	Show an awareness of change / Talk about what is seen and what is happening	Combine and repeat a range of movements / Sit up, stand up and balance on various parts of the body / Move in a range of ways, such as slithering, shuffling, rolling, crawling, walking, running, jumping, riding, skipping and hopping	Respond to sound with body movement / Begin to move rhythmically
Monday	Encourage children to sort out disputes independently	Cut, stick and sort letters from newspapers and magazines into alphabet book	Easter egg hunt clues – go through the tunnel over the stile / Clues to take children to shapes	Painting with large brushes and water / Digging using gardening tools / Books about tadpoles	Stage – dance routines / Apparatus: Assault course – use for clues in egg hunt / Mats for balancing / Skipping ropes / Quoits and poles for throwing	Stage and tape player / Jack's house role-play area / Sign posts
Tuesday	→		Start up egg hunt / Find shapes by clues about shapes' properties	Move pond to near log pile	Enlarge stage apparatus as before – encourage use of positional vocabulary to describe movements / Water – ripping paper	→
Wednesday	→	Write names on the list for dances	Continue egg hunt →	Digging – gardening tools →	Stage – more variety of music incorporate balances into egg hunt →	→
Thursday	→	Focus on name writing skills		Observe mushrooms and seeds planted →	→	
Friday	→		Remaining children to do egg hunt			

Children for focus: All children to be involved in egg hunt. Donna and Beth to take it in turns (five at a time).

Figure 2.8 Example of a week's plan, from Southmead Primary School

Evaluation (Green/Brown)

	Personal, social and emotional development	Communication, language and literacy development	Mathematical development	Knowledge and understanding of the world	Physical development	Creative development
Monday	Circle time: discussed how we could sort out our disputes.	Khahd and Khadijah asked if they could stick the letters on their books.		Rhys working with soil: 'Mix up the potion to make a bat.'	Children enjoyed obstacle course. Reece asked for mats to be added. David achieved his first handstand.	Stage was very successful. Children wrote their names on list. David did some fantastic moves.
Tuesday	Continued to encourage children to resolve disputes by talking about what was wrong.	No space for newspaper letters. Wrote names on dance list instead. Focused on children's next steps, e.g. learning next letter.	Donna used positional/directional clues for egg hunt. Children found shapes from clues about properties of shape.	Lots of social skills in use with soil tray – sharing equipment and taking turns.	Children worked in groups for dancing. Some groups (particularly reception girls) developing dance routines and extending them throughout the course of the day. Keyna very dominant as was Nasmah. Emaan keeps saying she's a boy.	Good responses to music. Children dances developed throughout the day. Jack's house just used as role-play home.
Wednesday	Louie and Tuisan sorted out their own dispute.	Dean wrote a perfect 'D' and 'n'. Children eager to record their names.	Zara was not very confident balancing. Needed lots of encouragement.	Sienna and Liban filled up the soil hole. 'Look we mended it!' – Sienna.	Emaan really enjoyed dancing.	
Thursday		Connor wrote his name perfectly. Children becoming more confident writing names.	Children found shapes from clues about properties. Generally good knowledge of 2D shapes.	Some children (Duncan and Shanon) enjoyed tipping out flower pots.	Bradley obsessed with Michael Jackson. Understanding about writing name on list and waiting his turn.	Children worked well in groups for dances.
Friday		→	→	→	Dancing still popular. Remaining children finished egg hunt. Apparatus used by others.	→

Figure 2.9 Example of activity and child evaluation at the end of a week, from Southmead Primary School

Setting up

Having a good outdoor area inevitably means there will be more work for the staff to do. However, it is possible to cut the workload, by thinking about children setting up some of the activities themselves and having the storage arranged so they can access the equipment (see Figure 2.10). Trolleys or boxes can be used to keep equipment in, which can either be kept *in situ* under the veranda as in Figure 2.11, or on wheels as in Figures 2.12 and 2.13. Boxes are easy as they can be simply lifted out and placed on the ground, for children to access when they want, as in Figure 2.14. DIY stores produce sheds of various sizes and shapes that can be used as in Figure 2.15 to house an imaginative scene, here a café, or for the construction equipment or blocks (see Figure 2.41). All the adult needs to do is unlock the padlock and bring out housed equipment such as the café chairs and table. In these ways setting up can become much less time consuming and children can access resources as they wish in a workshop environment.

Figure 2.10 Clearly labelled boxes

Figure 2.11 Woodwork resources readily available

Figure 2.12 Bats and balls in trolley

Figure 2.13 Building and construction materials

Part of the reason we set up the equipment is to give starting points to children, as they may be unsure as to what they can do or want to do. Therefore an interesting arrangement of equipment or a collection of resources can be the key to starting the play going. Likewise, photographs can offer starting points for children (see Figure 2.16).

Playing with children

There is a fine line between playing with children and interfering in their play and learning. Children do need time to play purposefully without adults; they need a level of freedom to work things out for themselves and between themselves. At these times the adult needs to be in a supervisory role, so that possible problems can be averted, for example slippery shoes on the metal climbing apparatus. However, children need to know that when they need an adult they can access one (see Figure 2.17) and likewise the adults will have specific children they wish to work with, and they can take advantage of those incidental times during play to do this.

Figure 2.14 A box of clipboards

Figure 2.15 A café in a shed

Figure 2.16 Photographs placed outside

There are good reasons for joining in with children's play:

learning increases

the quality of play and conversation improves

the status of the play and activity is raised

the self-esteem of those involved is raised

unsure children can be supported and

stereotypical play can be reduced.

Figures 2.18–2.28 demonstrate some of the roles adults take on.

Fine tuning

According to McLean (1991) not only does the adult need to work with and alongside children, they also need to keep a watchful eye on all that is going on to ensure the environment works effectively for all (see Figures 2.29–2.31). Staff need to:

manage the time and space

add to a play situation

give ideas

Figure 2.17 Staff member explaining the story

add resources

make sure the play of one group does not encroach on another

pre-empt problems

encourage children to try out new skills and ideas

stop children giving up

make connections for children

ensure children have choices

make sure the space doesn't become too messy and therefore useless.

Figure 2.18 Posing ideas

Figure 2.19 Pointing out

Teaching

Children need time away from adults, but they also need input, which enables them to think and develop. Such input are aspects of teaching, including providing opportunities, challenge, stimulation and progression, and consideration of the importance of observation, a suitable adult rota, safety issues and involving children in the tidying up.

Opportunity

Adults make things possible for children, by providing the right environment, the right resources and the right ethos, which says 'have a go'. Figures 2.31 and 2.32 involved half an hour of construction for these children, in which the adult was always around, ready to help if necessary, giving pointers where appropriate. The two main characters ended up working together. At one point a group of children collected a carpet to help the constructions keep stable. These children had resources and could access more; they could 'have a go'. Figure 2.33 offers open-ended opportunities – some children could write a magic potion recipe, some could imagine and mix it.

Case study

Boys were misusing milk crates, throwing them about and so on. Rather than point the finger at the children the staff decided to see if it was the fault of what equipment was available and how it was being provided. So they put netting over the milk crates, added Action Man dolls and Lego base plates and the play was transformed. Children played intensive action adventures, involving lots of talk, negotiation and humour.

Figure 2.20 Developing language

Figure 2.21 Demonstrating and encouraging

Challenge

By asking challenging questions or posing challenging situations, adults will enable children to really think. Figure 2.34 involved pulling up a bucket full of stones; it took many attempts and various numbers of children to be successful. In Figure 2.35 there are three buckets with hard-ended skipping ropes attached and threaded through the fence. These were home-made pulleys, and the children had to think, try out and adapt in the light of their findings as they raised various objects. Figure 2.36 is about making a workable see-saw, a child-initiated game. A challenge for one child may not be for another; you need to know your children to really offer true challenge. In Figure 2.37 matching the numbered ticket collected at the front of the bus with the correct seat was challenging for this child.

Stimulation

Children need to be interested in what they are doing, and need a reason for doing it; stimulation increases motivation, motivation increases perseverance and perseverance increases the likelihood of understanding.

Figure 2.22 *Developing motor skills*

Figure 2.23 *Discussing and negotiating*

A recent study into secondary-school boys noted that boys were more affected than girls by how interesting lessons were. 'Teachers who were best at motivating boys were those who used humour and real-life situations' (Shaw 2003). Activities need to be fun and involve real life.

Case study

A child found some fungi in the nursery garden and this set off an interest that involved another child. Figure 2.38 is a record of the observations made by the adult and the development of various ideas. These two children were fascinated by their discovery and the adult, May, could easily have made it a one-day interest and then dropped it, but instead she developed the activity to include drawing, writing, sign making, scientific discovery and care for others.

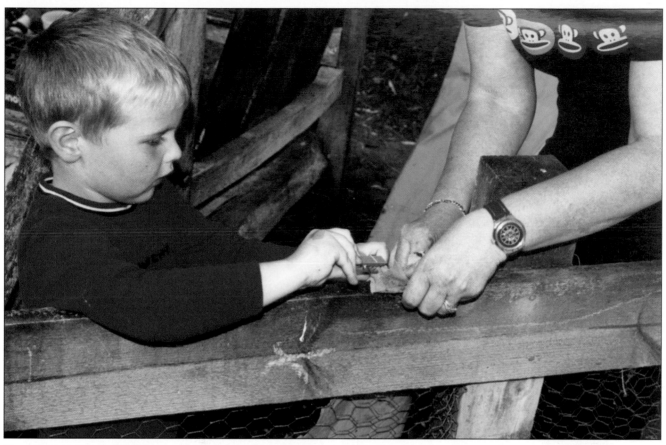

Figure 2.24 Helping and holding

Figure 2.25 Supporting the play of a number of children

Figure 2.26 Raising the status of play

Figure 2.27 Being there

Figure 2.28 Friendship

Figure 2.29 An adult suggested setting up a list to avoid arguments about who was next to play tennis

Figure 2.30 An adult stands close by, in case the children cannot sort out the disagreement

Figure 2.31 Adding a carpet to help keep the ground flat for the constructions

Figure 2.32 Half an hour of concentrated play

Figure 2.33 Big and small pans, spoons, gloves plus treasure for the magic potion

Figure 2.34 Working together to solve a problem

Figure 2.35 Experimenting with home-made pulleys

Progression

To help children and to teach them we need to know where we are going with them and what it is we are expecting by the time they leave us. Mathematical and linguistic development is fairly well known, there is an order and progression and knowledge about skills to be learnt. However, I am not sure the same applies to other areas, for example physical or creative development. Below is a list of motor skills children need to attain:

* **Locomotor**, or gross motor, **development** is about moving through the environment, which involves large movement patterns, such as: *walking, running, jumping, hopping, skipping, sliding, leaping, climbing, crawling, standing, sitting.*

* **Non-locomotor development** or stabilising maintaining equilibrium is about balancing, such as: *bending, stretching, twisting, pivoting, swinging, rolling, landing, stopping, dodging, balancing, inverted supports (upside down).*

* Manipulative or **fine motor skills** and **hand–eye** and **foot–eye co-ordination skills** are about imparting force on objects, such as: *throwing, catching, kicking, trapping, striking, volleying, bouncing, rolling, pulling, pushing, punting, grasping, reaching, gripping, holding, sewing, cutting, typing, writing, drawing, painting.*

(Bilton 2004)

However, for each motor skill the list of permutations is large. For example throwing – one can throw hard or soft, high or low, under or over arm, throw while running, throw from a horizontal position, throw backwards or forwards, throw and bounce. Do we seriously take into consideration the huge number of permutations to one motor skill and thereby teach all the skills? I am not expecting all five-year-olds to dive, catch a ball and throw it to someone else accurately. However, I would

Figure 2.36 Levers – making a see-saw

Figure 2.37 Matching numbers

32

James and Kamal: scientific development, plus other points (22 Nov 02)

James found toadstools in the garden. He became very interested in them and we looked up information about them in our library. James also asked his mother to take him to Balham library to find out more.

His enthusiasm made Kamal interested too. The boys went on a toadstool hunt as they had discovered that toadstools could be poisonous and dangerous to touch. They found three different types of toadstools in different parts of the garden. During this exercise the boys used the digital camera to take photos of the toadstools.

They drew pictures of the toadstools. Kamel held the pen half-way down in an almost triangular grip. He was shown how to hold it in a full triangular grip and needed reminding to hold it correctly. James initially used a palm grasp (not successfully) and needed help to start to use a triangular grip. During the session he did try to use the triangular grip but did say frequently that he couldn't draw or write. Lots of encouragement was needed for James to attempt to draw. When it came to making the warning signs he again said he couldn't draw and Kamal helped him. James and Kamel drew and made signs warning children not to touch the toadstools. These signs were designing and making something for a purpose. The boys drew round their hands, and then drew a red cross through these to warn children not to touch them (caring for others). We discussed how and where to put the signs; Kamal asked what would happen if it rained, he said the paper would get 'all wet and wasted' (knowledge of water on materials).

James knew about putting paper in plastic sheets to protect them, he thought this might also work with the signs. The boys helped each other manoeuvre the paper into the plastic sheets, then put tape at the end to stop the sheet falling out. The next problem was how to attach the signs to the trees (decided by the boys). They both decided to nail the sheets to the trees where the toadstools were growing.

This whole exercise was self-initiated and showed lots of negotiation and co-operative skills between the two.

Figure 2.38 Discovery of some toadstools that acted as a stimulus

Week beginning: *10 March*   Base: *Garden*

Day of the week	Morning		Morning	Afternoon		Afternoon
	Focused activity	Evaluation	Focused activity	Focused activity	Evaluation	
Monday	Provision: *Water the tree pots, teaspoons and water* Purpose: *Imaginative mixing*	Children transporting water in teaspoons and dribbling water into tree trunk. Described as 'decorating tree' make a house'. One child brought hay cart over for the 'house'. They collected more water when pots empty.	Provision: *Cars and gutters* Purpose: *K & U - ramps/levels* *Maths - measures*		Lots of talk of measurement – fast/slow, further/longer. Discussions on which cars went faster and why and further and why. Mainly boys.	
Tuesday	Provision: *Looking at patterns in the garden* Purpose: *K & U* *Patterns/sequences maths*	Changed to dribbling water down bark of beech tree. Children used pipettes and syringes. Lots of interest in the routes the water took. Children felt texture of bark, was it different wet/dry? Lots of discussion.	Provision: *Bark rubbings* Purpose: *K & U - texture* *Creative - technique*		Supply teacher made Post It observations on children. Focus kept some children very interested, other children drifted. Magic potions still very popular so this tended to have sustained work.	
Wednesday	Provision: *Water painting* Purpose: *Mark making* *communication, literacy and language, Social*	Very popular activity which involved wide range of children from those who don't usually mark make to those who do all the time – lots of expressive movements, large and small, working together to cover concrete area. Children maintained focus for a long period of time.	Provision: *Tues aims looking at patterns* Purpose: *Looking for patterns in the garden, use of digital camera - ICT*		R used camera well and saw lots of patterns – confident use of camera, but didn't want to give it up to other children. S enjoyed looking as did D. D lost interest quickly in the patterns, really just appeared to want to hold camera.	
Thursday	Provision: *More challenging climbing frame and planks* Purpose: *Physical challenge, Physical work co-ordination*	Some children very confident and able using planks and climbing frame. Moved planks and barrel near climbing frame to encourage children to try different moves. Popular with children who really enjoyed this. Simple arrangement still available for less confident children.	Provision: *Challenging physical play Climbing frame* Purpose: *Extend equipment, Large motor co-ordination, Hand-eye co-ordination challenge*		Children enjoyed the challenge at the horizontal plank. It may be an idea to make a really long plank by using A-frame to join with planks. Or more challenging slides going down or maybe invest in some new A-frames.	
Friday	Provision: *Magic potions* Purpose: *Maths Measurement -* *full/empty* *How much more?*	Lots of interest as in the digging area – some recipes set out and children collected clipboards and paper to make own recipes. Different groups used area all through morning – use as focus for counting next week.	Provision: Purpose:			

Figure 2.39 Evaluation based on observations of the activities that take place outside each day at Balham Nursery School

Figure 2.40 Working alongside children but at the same time making observational notes (Red nose day – hence Claire's wig!)

Figure 2.41a Children tidying up without an adult helping, but the adult was present in case help was needed

Figure 2.41b, c Children tidying up without an adult helping, but the adult was present in case help was needed

expect that we would be teaching children so that they can throw a ball in a variety of ways by the time they leave us and that we should have some idea about what we could expect from each age range.

Observation

Outside, as inside, we need to make observations of children and make judgements about the resources and environment we have provided. Figure 2.40 shows an adult working alongside children to answer questions and support the reading, but at the same time making observational notes on specific children. The children are not adversely affected by the adult writing and it gives children a very clear role model to demonstrate a reason for writing.

Figure 2.9 shows assessment of actual activities and of children having used the equipment, linking to the plans in Figure 2.8 at Southmead Primary School. Figure 2.39 is an evaluation based on observations of the activities that take place outside each day at Balham Nursery School. It discusses children's learning and how materials were used and looks to future provision. Note how the focus is different in the afternoon to cater for the children who attend all day and the range of curriculum areas covered for the focus.

Figure 2.42 Children have been shown how to fold correctly and so could do it without adult help

Adult rota

It is preferable to have as flexible a rota as possible so that staff are not outside for the whole session, otherwise it can end up with staff wilting on a hot day or freezing on a cold day. Likewise you may find a group of children an adult is working with want to go inside to continue some aspect of play and it needs the adult to be with them. With a flexible rota another member of staff can swap and go outside while that member continues to work with their group inside.

'Safeness'

I have called this section 'safeness' as I feel it describes more clearly than 'safety' what a safe environment is. Safety can often be seen as a rather narrow term and in a negative light. Physically the area has to be safe and not dangerous but not without risk and challenge. Stephenson (2003) argues that risk to a four-year-old is about attempting something new, feeling on the borderline of 'out of control' (often involving height and speed) and overcoming fear. She further argues that if you make an environment hazard free it becomes challenge free, and then 'children have less experience in making decisions on their own, less opportunity to assess their own personal frontiers and less opportunity to gain confidence and self-esteem through coping independently' (Stephenson 2003: 42). While we need to be aware of the negative effects of risk, we also need to focus on the positive effects, such as raised confidence, bravery, strength and success. All of us feel a sense of achievement if we complete something that for us feels risky. But 'safeness' is more than just about height and speed; it can also cover anything a child may feel is risky and for some this could be putting pen to paper, so we have to make sure the child feels safe to have a go at anything. 'Safeness' is about enabling things to happen, not shutting down opportunities.

To make a safe environment, think about the following:

Be aware of dangers in the setting and get rid of these problems.

Make a risk assessment of the outdoor area and check this regularly.

Make sure there is challenge.

Decide what clothing and footwear you feel is suitable for outside.

Discuss regularly with children 'safeness', risk and challenge.

Write a 'safeness' policy that can be passed on to the parents and carers.

Make sure the area is safe for all children to have a go at any activity.

Outside staff need to be ever watchful, even if they are engrossed in an activity with a particular group of children.

Tidying up

Children can tidy up, as long as they are shown how to, and they are given the guidelines. Figure 2.41 demonstrates this. The children were asked to tidy up, no one ran away and at one point there were nine children working together to get the blocks back into

Figure 2.43 Signals for tidy-up time

the shed. The children had been shown how to tidy up without an adult helping, but the adult was present in case help was needed. In Figure 2.42 the children are able to fold correctly because they have been shown how to do it.

Sometimes children need a variety of stimuli to move on to another activity. In Figure 2.43 the children hear a bell at tidy-up time, a member of staff says 'It is tidy-up time,' and holds up a sign which reads 'tidy up'.

Questions

Look at your practice. Is any stereotypical behaviour going on? What is causing it? Can you change the environment to stop this behaviour?

We are all guilty of assuming that how we should do something is how we actually do it and that the plans match what we actually do in practice, but this is often not the case! Are *all* the adults in the setting working with *all* the children and working at *all* the activities?

Do you ever recreate a play scene from the day before? Could you think about doing this, thereby extending the play?

Are observations of children outside shared with parents in the same way as activities inside?

Can adults get involved in play that enables the children to take control and take the lead?

Chapter 3
The outdoor play curriculum

In this chapter I will be looking at how to offer the whole curriculum in the outdoor area (Figure 3.1 shows children busy outside at woodwork, covering several aspects of the curriculum).

Figure 3.1 *Woodwork involves use of mathematics, science, creativity, motor skills, language, accuracy, perseverance – the list is endless*

Any educational setting will divide the area up into areas, zones or bays and outside is no different. How you arrange this or list it will be to an extent up to you, as long as you cover the nine areas of learning and experience as detailed by the DES (1989), namely:

Linguistic and literary

Aesthetic and creative

Human and social

Mathematical

Moral

Physical

Scientific

Technological

Spiritual.

I will organise this chapter under the learning bays, but you may decide to organise it differently. For example Edgington (2003) lists the following:

a climbing area

space to run

a wheeled vehicle area

space to develop skills with small equipment

a quiet area

places to hide

a wild area

an area for large-scale construction and imaginative play

space for play with natural material

a gardening area.

The Gloucestershire Outdoor Learning guidance (Edwards and Fee 2003) lists the following areas:

Physical

Natural

Social

Manipulative and creative

Role play

Transition.

Or you could divide it by how children work and play, which are:

Imaginative play

Design and construction

Communication and language

Investigation and exploration.

The areas or learning bays I suggest for outside are the:

Imaginative play bay

Building and construction bay

Gymnasium bay

Small apparatus bay

Horticultural bay

Environmental and scientific bay

Art bay

Quiet bay.

Whatever way you divide the area you may like to think about the following:

* If you list actual equipment, for example 'climbing frame, house, monkey bars', you may find that you see each piece of equipment as only being able to provide for one curriculum area, whereas the climbing frame could be used as a den or as a scaffold to hold equipment for a science experiment.

* In the same way if you zone space, then equipment does not have to be static; sand could be used in the investigative area or it could be used in the imaginative area.

* Under each zone would come a variety of activities to fit the description. So for example, under 'designing and making' we would include technology, woodwork and painting.

* Think about what you want children to do when they use the various areas outside. We want children to think, imagine, design, construct, make, communicate, investigate, explore and move. These descriptions are wide, for example 'communicate' could be verbally, through drawings, writings, dance and/or music. Under 'imagine' we would want children to be creative, to invent, to be original. Thinking involves the ability to consider, ponder, deliberate, reflect and make judgements.

* Make sure children have plenty of opportunities to set up and run their own ideas.

* Make sure all areas or zones accommodate children playing together and alone.

Imaginative play bay

Resources

A-frames

planks – commercially made and cut to order by a DIY store

ladders

cubes

heavy pieces of material

plastic sheeting/tarpaulin

wheeled toys – trucks, pushchairs, prams, carts, wheelbarrows (see Figures 3.2 and 3.3 and Resources and contacts for details of suppliers of such trucks)

plastic crates – bread, milk, supermarket

blocks – wooden and plastic

large cardboard boxes

industrial tubing

cable spools (a variety of sizes up to one metre in diameter)

tree trunk sections

pieces of carpet and carpet squares

tents

large cones

broom handles – a broom handle dropped into a large cone, or parasol base filled with sand or set in a tub of cement, can be used to attach a sign to, or to drape material over to form a den, sun shade, or to attach a washing line between two (see Figure 3.4)

hose pipe – cut to lengths for fire fighter equipment and for sand and water play

imaginative props – for example a collection of props around a particular occupation (see Figures 3.5 and 3.6)

Figure 3.2 Truck with removable sides

Figure 3.3 Truck with detachable bike

Figure 3.4 *A broom handle used to attach a sign for the bus stop*

clothes including a huge selection of bags and hats

holiday equipment – backpacks, sleeping bags, cooking stuff, suitcases, picnic bags

builder's tools and equipment – mallets, screwdrivers, spirit levels, pulleys

DIY tools and tool belts

mechanic tools

decorator's tools – brushes, pots

ropes and pegs – the rope is a most versatile resource, for example it can be used for skipping, to attach a truck to a bike, made into a letter or number shape, formed into a circle to jump in and out of, laid out for balancing along and with a label attached it can become a petrol pump

gardening tools – shovels, spades, watering cans

home tools – cameras, mobile phones, personal stereos, binoculars, umbrellas, money, purses,
tickets, cards

fire fighter equipment (Figure 3.7)

doctor's bag and equipment

Figure 3.5 *Collection of props for a mechanic*

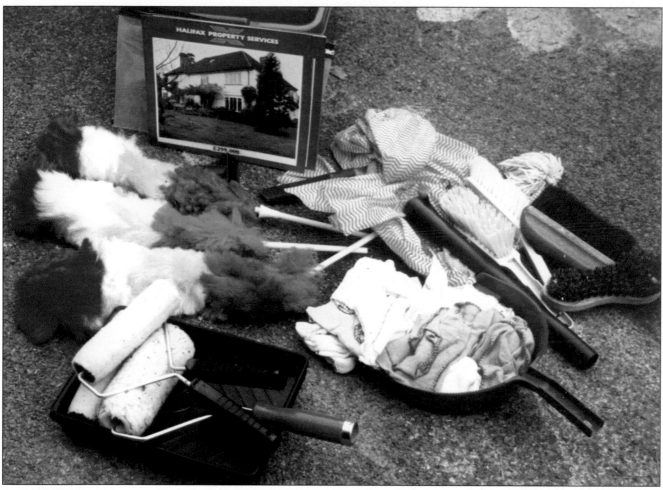

Figure 3.6 Collection of props for a window cleaner

Ideas

Garden centre

Boat

Pirate ship

Post office

Sorting office

Pizza delivery and pizza shop

Supermarket delivery depot and shop

Flower delivery

Builder/plasterer

Organised sport/ dance event

Dinosaur land

Removals

TV repair and reception

Fairy-tale castle

Garage reception and repairs

Fire station and fire engine

Ice-cream seller

Library

Dispatch rider

Remember

* Link imaginative play scenes inside and out, for example activities associated with the story of *Tom and the Island of Dinosaurs* (by Ian Beck, Picture Corgi Books) were placed inside and out as shown in Figures 3.8–3.12.

* Inspire children by reading stories and providing relevant props as shown in Figures 3.8–3.12.

* Outdoors allows movement and play on a large scale.

* The resources are almost endless.

* Do involve the children in the choice and design of focused imaginative areas.

* Provide many imaginative areas. In real life we move from one situation to another, whether it be from the home to the shops, to work, to the library and so on; children need the same opportunities.

* Do provide imaginative play every day.

* Make sure children are able to set up their own imaginative games too.

Figure 3.7 Fire fighter equipment – ladder, plastic hat, braces, baggy home-made trousers, rope

Figure 3.8 The story of Tom and the Island of Dinosaurs *is read to the children*

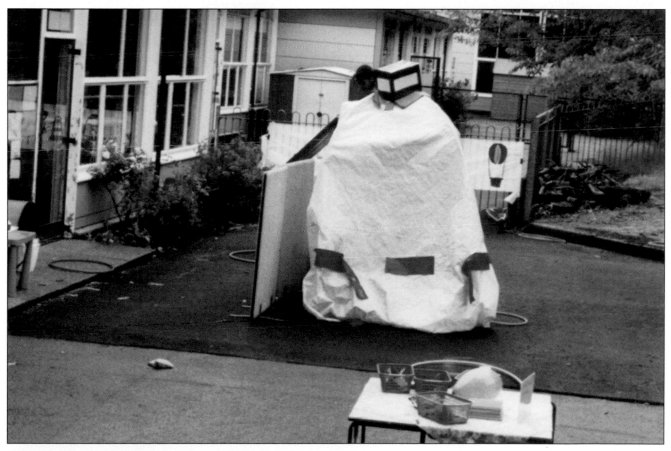

Figure 3.9 The climbing frame is made into a lighthouse

Figure 3.10 Table set up to write messages in a bottle

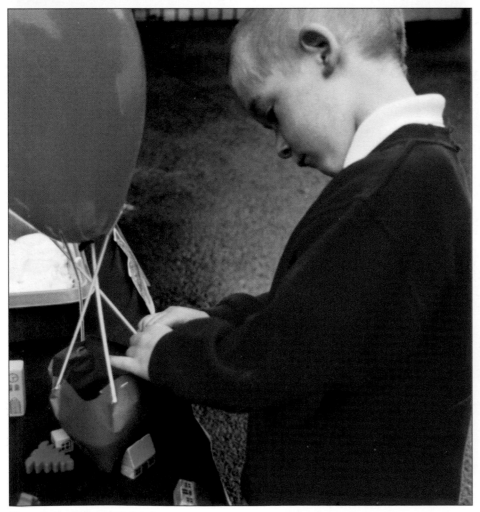

Figure 3.11 Making a hot air balloon

This setting liked to discuss with the children what imaginative areas they would like. On this occasion the children wanted a removals firm. Initially the staff found books and information on the subject, encouraging the families to do likewise. Children do not necessarily know a great deal about a particular occupation and so staff role-played typical removal scenes. For about a week there were discussions about the subject of moving house, storing furniture, the reasons for moving, distances travelled and so on. A variety of empty boxes were collected, plus a host of household items, and two houses were set up, one inside and one out, and so the removals started. Pull-along trunks had roofs attached using broom handles and a large piece of material. Each day the play was assessed, resources added and new activities set up. A real removal man came into the setting and talked to the children, and his funny stories were then used in their play! Significant from the play was the high level of negotiating skills (around furniture getting stuck and how furniture would fit together in a truck) and the improvement in spatial awareness, all this with lots of laughter.

Figure 3.12 *Table with various stages of the story*

Building and construction bay

Resources

A-frames

planks

cubes

crates

ladders

different sized cardboard boxes

cable spools (a variety of sizes up to one metre in diameter)

plastic tubing

any wooden blocks – non-standard, unit and hollow (see Figures 3.13 and 3.14 and Resources and contacts for details)

sanded wooden off-cuts

breeze blocks

bricks

Figure 3.13 *Nine trays of very small blocks*

material

funnels

a variety of containers, jugs and digging implements

DIY builders trays or large trays from stores such as IKEA

collections of:

stones

shells

twigs

pebbles

bark

cork

leaves

small logs

Figure 3.14 Treeblocks – parents of this child were concerned he could not draw a straight line, but look at the precision in this work

Figure 3.15 Building a den using cubes/boxes and material

Ideas

Building a tower using wooden off-cuts and mud.

Building a bridge using crates and planks.

Building a den using cubes/boxes and material (see Figure 3.15).

Building a construction using crates, guttering, funnels and jugs to move water from one place to another.

Digging a tunnel in the sand and supporting the sides with blocks, twigs and small logs.

Making patterns with logs, stones and embroidery rings.

Damming up the water flow, changing the course of flow using a waterspout and stones and pebbles, for example by using a fixed water feature as in Figure 3.16. This was well used by children – dropping objects including stones and planks, anticipating the change of flow, seeing if it could be dammed and enjoying water on a cold day.

Remember

* This area could include:

  building

  woodwork (see Figures 3.1, 3.17 and 3.18)

  sand and water play, not necessarily in trays and pits (see Figure 3.19)

  digging plot.

* This bay involves mathematical and linguistic development, including understanding of weight, density, volume, position and relationship of objects to each other. It will involve the language of negotiation, discussion, possibilities, why and if, and future ideas.

* Building and construction often leads to imaginative play (see Figure 3.20).

* You do not need to replicate provision. If there is sand outside, it does not have to be inside too. Think about having two sand areas outside, so that sand can be transported, but watch for sand on hard surfaces as it can become very slippery. Or have a small coal-bunker type shed, from a DIY store and fill it with sand so that it can be scooped out and used in play. Or use a piece of material for sand (see Figure 3.19).

* Give children the opportunities to work alone as well as together on projects (see Figure 3.19).

Figure 3.16 A fixed water feature, around one metre square, filled with large rocks with a water source in the middle

* Keep a project ongoing by setting it up the next day in the same way as the children left it the previous day.

* Use carpet squares or thick cardboard so children can sit on the ground even when it is damp and cold (see Figure 3.21).

* The digging area could include logs, stones, dinosaurs, small world figures for construction and imaginative play.

* Have hooks positioned around the outside area, so when one wants to attach or hold a rope, musical instrument, pulley or whatever, it can be done immediately.

Figure 3.17 Children using woodwork tools; woodwork is not dangerous if organised well and if children are trained how to use the equipment properly

Figure 3.18 An aeroplane made by the child, ready to test out

Figure 3.19 Sand on a piece of material, sanded wooden off-cuts, tractors and spades provide stimulating solitary play

Figure 3.20 Children started to build this square, which quickly became a house with cooker

Figure 3.21 Thick cardboard enables children to sit on the ground even when it is damp

Gymnasium bay

Resources

planks	ladders
A-frames	hoops
moveable climbing frame	half logs
boxes	carpet squares
crates	tyres
cubes	cones
barrels	canes
tunnels	ropes

trees and logs – Think about fund raising to buy trees to plant that in time will have grown large enough for climbing (see Figures 3.22 and 3.23).

'Monkey bars' – A thick rope secured between two posts will serve as a monkey bar (see Figure 3.24).

Ideas

Challenge children to move around the equipment without touching the ground.

Challenge children to move quickly, yet deliberately, like a particular animal.

Challenge children to think of as many ways as they can to get around the equipment.

Ask children to follow a sequence of letters or numbers.

Link up a number of gymnasium layouts.

Ask children to set up the equipment, so one stays as close to the ground as possible.

Remember

∗ Obstacle courses are for children to work on alone or with friends, not in competition with each other.

∗ Allow children to set up the arrangement of equipment themselves (see Figure 3.25).

∗ This bay is about developing physical activity and physical skills – balance, co-ordination and strength.

∗ Children need plenty of opportunities to practise, modify and refine their movements in order to reach a mature pattern of movement and high level of self-confidence.

∗ Adults need to offer guidance, support and encouragement.

∗ Adults need to be aware of what skills they are hoping children will gain and not expect children to 'catch' the learning.

∗ Allow children to feel a sense of achievement by being able to take risks, try something new and/or overcome fear (see Figures 3.26–3.29). The child in Figure 3.27 is not as confident as the child in 3.26 but given the opportunity will be so.

∗ Appreciate and acknowledge what children are learning and can do (see Figure 3.30).

Figure 3.22 Trees can be climbed

Figure 3.23 Felled trees are an effective climbing apparatus for developing balancing skills

Figure 3.24 'Monkey bars' are good for the strengthening of shoulder, arm, hand and finger muscles

Figure 3.25 Children have set up this arrangement themselves

Figure 3.26 No hands

Figure 3.27 Going across rather tentatively, but a great sense of achievement once across

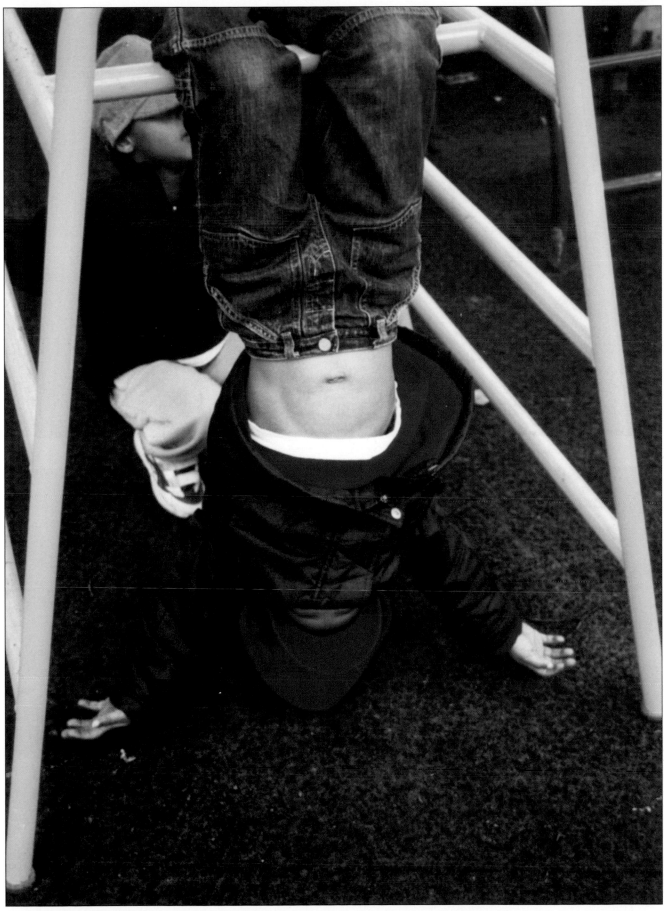

Figure 3.28 Hanging upside down not holding on with hands

Figure 3.29 Upside down, holding on with two feet and one hand, using the other hand to pick up a hat

Figure 3.30 The level of hand–eye and foot–eye co-ordination is high to do this manoeuvre

Small apparatus bay

Resources

balls – various sizes, weights and materials

bats – various

hoops – various sizes

bean bags – (except in the wet as they get very heavy)

equipment and resources from other bays

Ideas

Aiming at targets (see Figures 2.22 and 3.31)

Hook the duck

Hoopla

Rolling, estimating and measuring (see Figures 3.32 and 3.33)

Set up a game – bowling, tennis, golf. The tennis game shown in Figure 3.34 was set up during Wimbledon fortnight. The net was plastic tape strung between a cone and the fence. Children had to write up the games and sets they scored. There was a huge amount of interest and the quality of play was high. There was also a table set up with a computer and writing materials.

Figure 3.31 Throwing the dice, then having to throw the right number of bean bags into the correct numbered circle

Figure 3.32 Rolling the cable spool along a piece of paper, marking and measuring the distance travelled

Figure 3.33 Using an A-frame, guttering and balls to estimate and compare which will be the fastest

Figure 3.34 This tennis game was set up during Wimbledon fortnight

Remember

* Combine the more formal curriculum with motor skill development. This can often encourage children who are reticent about reading and writing (see Figures 3.31 and 3.34).

* This area can get out of hand, so think of ways of containing balls (see Figure 3.35).

* You do not need lots of fancy and expensive equipment. Just attach an opened coat hanger to a sturdy object for a basketball net and use boxes on the ground to aim into.

* Allow children to set up their own games. Figure 3.36 shows such a game where the children have made a train using three hoops. There is skill in holding on to the hoop and keeping the train intact, involving co-operation and careful timing of movements.

Figure 3.35 Containing a tennis ball inside tights or a stocking tied to a washing line avoids balls getting lost

Figure 3.36 Children making up their own game – a train using three hoops

Horticultural bay

Resources

ground or any kind of container for growing

child size and adult size:

spades	seeds
trowels	plants
forks	camera
gardening gloves	writing and drawing materials
wheelbarrows	
watering cans	water butt/outside tap – so children can collect water when they want and it can be used in any part of the outside area.
hoses	
plant pots	
canes	

Ideas

From September onwards plant bulbs for a spring show, for example daffodils, tulips and crocuses.

In May, after the last frosts, plant the following for a summer and early autumn show:

corms, bulbs and tubers, for example anemones, freesia, iris, *Liatris spicata* and dahlias

vegetables, for example beans, carrots, peas, marrows, potatoes (also the early variety), lettuce, cucumber and tomatoes (see Figure 3.37)

annuals, for example cosmos, marigolds and petunias

hardy annual seeds, for example alyssum, *Asperula* species, candytuft, clarkia, clary, lavatera, *Limnanthes* species, nasturtium, scabious and Virginia stock.

Plant evergreen zones, same colour plant zones, smelly zones and texture zones.

Figure 3.37 July – tomatoes, lettuce, carrots, cucumber

Figure 3.38 A very hot summer – children needed to water these annuals every morning and afternoon

Remember

* This bay is about planting, tending and harvesting, not planting, forgetting to tend and dying. Do not attempt this activity if it is not going to be seen through (see Figure 3.38).

* You do not have to be an expert gardener but this area does need thoughtful planning.

* Children need to record the life cycle in words, drawings, photographs, collage, paint, computer-generated graphs and any other medium possible.

* This area is about beauty, comparison and change.

* Plant heights can be measured, crops can be weighed, textures and smells compared, crops and petals counted.

* Make books charting the development of the plants. This is useful to encourage reading, writing and mathematical work with those children who are reticent about such things. Making labels and writing up rotas will also help with writing skills (see Figures 3.39 and 3.40).

* This bay would benefit from some form of low boundary fence or layer of bricks, so children appreciate this is a working environment and is not for play purposes.

Figure 3.39 Sophie's label for the tomatoes

Figure 3.40 Prompts to encourage the children to chart the development of their plants

* Children can be part of the planning process – looking forward to what jobs will need to be done next in the garden.

* Think very carefully about when the cycle will be complete, to ensure children do not leave before they have seen and tasted the fruits of their labour.

* Draw children's attention to the plants. Just because we notice things doesn't mean a child has done so (see Figure 3.41).

Figure 3.41 Really looking at and appreciating flowers

Case study

In September a setting in Norfolk planted bulbs around the outline of the tallest child. When the bulbs came through children were able to lie inside the outline of bulbs and were quite enclosed by the tall leaves and stalks. They could view the sky from a horizontal position and view the plants close up.

Environmental and scientific bay

Resources

environments for:

 birds (boxes, feeding tables, water baths, trees)

 animals (wild area)

 minibeasts (tree trunk sections, old carpet, large stones or evergreen cuttings)

 fish and amphibians (water) (see Figure 3.42).

 bats (boxes)

collecting pots

magnifying glasses

drawing and writing materials

gathering jars, also sheets to collect insects from trees and paint brushes for picking up invertebrates

pond dipping equipment

nets

weather boxes

camera

Ideas

A project on minibeasts or insects or invertebrates or an aspect of the weather could start from this bay.

A project focusing on close observational drawing.

A project involving difference, for example use of Venn diagrams.

Weather boxes, an idea from Marjorie Ouvry's (2000) book, suggests making up boxes of collections for each weather feature, namely wind, sun, snow, rain, and also frost and fog. Into these boxes put songs, rhymes, stories, poems, photographs, pictures, taped sounds, ideas and resources for experiments. Children could add ideas, their own drawings, poems and stories. It is very important to decide what you are trying to achieve and enable children to learn before you collect the resources. So for example with rain, it would be about the various levels of rain, from light to heavy, the channels rain will take once it's on the ground, the quantity of rain, the study of clouds and the effect of rain. Equally it needs to be about enjoying rain and being able to be in it while being protected from it (see Figure 5.4). We can also create weather features to experiment with (see Figure 3.43).

Pour water on an area of grass/soil and wait for the worms to come up. Use a sand timer to see how long it takes for them to appear and then disappear.

Remember

* This bay does not have to take up a great deal of space.

* With the children make books or laminated cards that specifically identify the organisms in their garden.

* This is a bay about valuing the organisms in our area, not grown ups being frightened of worms (see Figure 3.44).

* One has to be knowledgeable and be able to point out the difference between for example a centipede and a millipede.

* Make children aware of what is around; children can only notice and behave amazed if they are taught to.

* This will involve both informal discoveries and actual planned projects.

Figure 3.42 An old water tray transformed into a pond

Case study

Norcot Nursery takes photographs using a digital camera, prints them up with a caption, puts them on card and asks children to take the card into the garden and find the new thing or the change that has occurred. It may be the growth of a flower, the emergence of stems from the ground, a new insect or animal.

Figure 3.43 Creating rain to hear the sound and find out what angle the umbrella has to be at to protect the body

Figure 3.44 An endangered species – a stag beetle

Art bay

Resources

charcoal	boards to lean on
pastels	board for oil painting
oil paints	paper (thick and thin)
clay	sand
chalks	natural materials

Ideas

Group painting, that is, painting together at the same time, for example using a very large round piece of paper, divided into, say, eight sections, each eighth to be used by one child. It sounds strange but works very well!

Large or small pieces of paper taped to the ground or to the fence (see Figure 3.45).

Foot printing and hand printing (see Figure 3.46).

Figure 3.45 Children periodically came up and painted a picture on the paper attached to the fence

Figure 3.46 Foot printing

Figure 3.47 Art ephemera

Figure 3.48 Mosaic work, creating a beautiful spot

No worries about mess.

Observational drawings of specific plants that the setting has grown.

Clay using no tools – How many ways can it be touched (poked/thumped/stroked/clawed/squashed/rolled etc.)?

Sand and water sculptures.

Art ephemera, either on the ground (see Figure 3.47) or using the fence to weave and attach.

Make bookmarks using double-sided sellotape on thin card to stick flowers, leaves etc.

Create permanent art outside (see Figure 3.48).

Case study

Gary did not like mess, on his body or clothes, and he avoided dough, clay, paint, mud and so his involvement with art materials was quite limited. One day foot printing was offered outside. Gary watched and eventually took his shoes and socks off and did indeed do some foot printing. After that he used any and all 'messy' materials and never looked back. We need to 'catch' all the children whatever It takes,

Remember

* Drawing is about communicating and making sense of ideas and feelings. Adams (2003: 4) argues that drawing is an artistic and recreational activity but also an intellectual one. Make sure children have constant access to drawing materials, whether it be chalking on the ground or drawing on a piece of cardboard. Value drawing by remembering it is as important as writing (see Figure 3.49 – this drawing arose from the play based on a cat stuck up a tree discussed in Chapter 1 and shown in Figure 1.1).

* All famous artists have created pictures outside.

* Outside gives a different light and shadow to inside (see Figure 3.50).

Figure 3.49 *The cat up the tree*

* Outside mess does not matter as much as inside – so use the more messy resources such as charcoal outside.

* Outside is a far better place to do an observational picture because it provides a greater level of inspiration.

* Art is about me, not about someone else's ideas.

* Add seeds from the pet shop and feathers (baked in the oven to kill germs) for art ephemera.

* Dark corners outside can create very good reflections.

Figure 3.50 *The shadow on this paper gave a very different feel to this roller painting*

Quiet bay

Resources

carpet squares, material, chairs, cushions	dictaphones
	soft toys
tape recorder	language and mathematics games which cannot be blown by the wind
tapes – songs, stories, rhymes, sound games	
books – reference and fiction	small motor-skill games
comics and child magazines	writing and drawing materials

Remember

* Some children find it easier to look at books, write and so on, outside.

* This area will need adult input just as any other area does.

* Children can use the chalks whenever and wherever they want.

* Regularly change what is in the box.

* Dictaphones are good for encouraging children to speak and to speak to an audience. They can report on what is going on outside, similar to a TV presenter.

Other bays

Outside can be used for just about any activity. These could include:

story telling

singing

music (see Figures 3.51–3.53)

music and movement

meal times

snack (see Figures 3.54 and 3.55)

Case study

Legh Vale Early Years and Childcare Centre have moved from a formal to a play-based learning environment in the reception unit. The project has been going for two years and has involved and still involves a lot of work and a committed team. They looked at how children play, categorised play and set up play areas (role play, construction, mark making, water, sand, workshop, malleable, music, painting, book, IT, snack bar) and all were developed both inside and out. A lot of thought was put into where to place things. Children are able to move resources between play areas. Parents have expectations for their children and the provision on offer; learning is fun for children and adults. Child-initiated play is well done; it is not a free for all and there are targeted teaching times. As Edgington (2003) argues, child-initiated activities will be discouraged if we do not do them well. The Centre feels the project has been a great success and children are exceeding the Early Learning Goals for all areas of learning, confirmed by HMI and Ofsted.

(This case study was provided by J. Robinson and J. Potter in their workshop 'Moving from a formal to a play-based learning environment in a reception year unit' at the Institute of Education Early Years Conference 7 July 2003.)

Figure 3.51 Commercially made instruments

Figure 3.52 Musical mobiles using bamboo, metal, lids and wooden spoons

Figure 3.53 The house made into a music corner so children could make music together

Figure 3.54 *Water ready for children to serve themselves*

Questions

Do the outdoor activities enable children to become involved in representing their ideas in a written form?

Are children encouraged to plan their play for the next day and predict what will happen next in the activity?

Are children encouraged to listen to each other?

Are children encouraged to use mathematical language in a precise way as they work?

Are you mathematically literate?

Are children encouraged to make pre- and post-plans of their constructions?

What do you do for the children who tend to play with a limited number of activities? Does it matter?

Is the storage area safe so children can use equipment and resources as they wish?

Figure 3.55 *Even though this was a really cold day some children wanted to drink their milk outside*

Chapter 4
Creating a workable playing environment

In this chapter I will be looking at the environment, the 'how' of the educational equation, particularly time, space, resources and adults. The how of education brings children and curriculum together, but done badly the how part of the equation can undo any good work you are trying to achieve. Constantly we need to evaluate what we are putting in, in terms of effort and money, and decide whether we are reaping enough rewards from that effort; if not things need to change.

Figure 4.1 A covered way so children can play outside whatever the weather

Resources

How you arrange resources and what you make available to the children says a lot about what sort of practitioners you are. If children cannot access resources freely this suggests you do not trust them. If there are very few resources, you do not care about them. If children are not allowed to mix resources and equipment you do not want them to think. For children to think through and follow up ideas they need to be able to put their thoughts into actions, so if they need the blocks, plus cones, broom handles, material and some large leaves to make an idea in their head real, they should be able to do this. In a home where play is valued, children will gather resources from many areas – bathroom, kitchen, living room, garden. Haworth, Desforges and Orgill (1992), looking into play in school home corners, found that the accessibility of resources was important in enhancing children's learning. Where children could select resources they were able to make informed choices, make decisions and have control over the direction of play and this in turn improved the quality of play and learning. Free and found resources are about the most useful, with a scattering of bought ones. (Figure 2.1 shows balsa wood being used as sandwiches.) (Try Scrapstores – www.childrens-scrapstore.co.uk for recycled leftovers.) Looking through the images in this book will demonstrate this; some of the pictures will show resources that have cost nothing.

Bikes

Three-wheeler bikes can cause more trouble than they are worth. The following is a description of what typically happens in a setting where bikes are used, particularly if outside play is allocated a set short period of time half-way through the session. Children who wish to go on the bikes will want to get outside as fast as possible and may not get suitably dressed for the weather just so that they are out first. No one has said to the children that the blue bike is the best, the yellow bike not so good and if you are on the green bike, well you are just a lower form of life. But this seems to be the attitude that prevails in every setting where bikes are simply put out en masse and children are left to get on with them. The story continues with children trying to stay on the bikes for as long as possible, not willing to share. When a child is taken off a bike, they will spend all their time trying to get back on the bike. Children may even act immorally to get a bike back: pushing others out of the way, pretending they haven't had a turn on the bike already. Staff end up policing, by organising who has a turn next, who has been wronged and who should be punished. This behaviour occurs day after day after day.

This is poor, stereotypical play and needs to be stopped. What appears to be happening is that the high status toy gives high status to the owner, and so the child's self-esteem goes up. Children like bikes because of the speed, they enjoy the feeling of moving fast, the status it gives them and the fear feeling. When the bike has to be given up the child's self-esteem goes down, they can feel lost and their only redress is

to try and get on a bike again. There may be an analogy here with real cars; some people feel better behind the wheel of a car and their self-esteem goes up.

What can be done?

* Most importantly, raise children's self-esteem so it stays high and is not affected by the possession or not of a toy.

* Think about not having bikes.

* Have two-wheeler bikes. There is no reason why under fives shouldn't be able to learn the skill of riding a two-wheeler.

* When three-wheeler bikes are used, insist that children have to have a truck tied to it, or only buy three-wheeler bikes with attachments.

* Fit an old bike, without the wheels, to a heavy wooden frame and make an exercise bike.

* Set up play scenarios which involve bikes, for example fast food delivery, ice-cream 'van', flower delivery, super-market delivery, postman and so on.

* Make sure adults get involved with the children's play, providing ideas and extending what children can do. It is very difficult to hold a conversation with a child who is simply whizzing by.

* Plan carefully for outdoor play, offer a variety of activities and be outside for as long as possible each day.

* Harding (2002) looked into improving bike play in her own setting and made a number of suggestions. These include encouraging children to manage bike play themselves, adults planning for intervention in bike play, setting up more imaginative play, offering a range of size and type of vehicles so there is more choice and getting information from home about the opportunities for this type of play at home.

All weather access

Outdoor play is not a summer pursuit (see Figure 4.1). Poor weather can be used as an excuse not to go out, but all weather conditions can be exploited.

How can this be achieved?

* Change the attitude so that instead of 'It's raining so we can't go out,' have 'It's raining, great, how can we use this for the benefit of the children?' or 'compensate for the constraints, exploit the opportunities' (see Figures 4.2–4.6).

* Heavy rain is really the only weather feature that stops you going outside. Do not timetable outdoor play for a particular time, and then you can go out when it is not raining. Extreme cold and wind don't stop you going out, but may limit the amount of time outside.

* Keep boxes of spare clothing and footwear, such as wellington boots, coats for all types of weather (cold and wet), gloves, hats, caps and long-sleeved T-shirts (see Figures 4.4 and 4.8). Finding out which boots fit can be a great mathematical exercise (Figure 4.7).

* Explain to parents and keep explaining that children will be working outside and why.

* Have an all weather policy.

Figure 4.2 A wet day, but children are still free to go outside and activities had been set up including this old mangle

Figure 4.3 Marbling in the puddles

Figure 4.4 Ways of storing umbrellas

Figure 4.5 Curling

Figure 4.6 Curling, sledging, brushing, and sliding using tin lids

Figure 4.7 A great mathematical exercise: 'Which boots fit me?'

Case study

A setting in Norfolk wanted the door to outside open all the time, but didn't want the children to freeze inside, so they hung a heavy piece of thick velvet material at the outside door. Children were trained not to leave anything near the door and to be careful as they went through. It effectively kept the room warm.

* Put together a development plan for shade and shelter. This could involve making shelters from materials draped over A-frames or over four secured poles, or draped between a fence and some other structure. Large umbrellas and pop-up tents offer a degree of shelter. Plant trees and quick growing shrubs to provide shade. A reasonable sized tree should offer protection within three years. Consider having some form of more permanent shelter built, such as a veranda or pull-out shade or pergola covered in thick plastic, canvas or bamboo sheeting (see Figure 4.1).

* In very poor weather free access to the outside may not be suitable for all, but small groups can be taken out (see Figure 4.9).

* There needs to be a variety of surfaces outside, and although grass is very attractive one can have too much. Some settings seem to have areas that collect rainwater but these can be made less boggy by buying all weather materials. Alternatively, train children to wear wellingtons but clean them when they come inside.

Figure 4.8 Ways of storing wellington boots and umbrellas

Case study

Children are allowed to go out in the wet and mud, and incidentally learn how to walk on muddy grass without falling over, but are expected to clean the boots when they come in. The routine is that each foot with a boot on is placed in a bowl of soapy water, scrubbed down with a long-handled brush and then left to dry on the side. Children learn to step back into their shoes once the operation is complete. Children are capable of so much if we give them the opportunity.

Figure 4.9 Small groups going out in the bitter cold

* Make up weather boxes for wind, sun, rain, snow, etc. Collect together resources, such as books, songs and rhymes, which are relevant to that particular weather feature (see Chapter 3 Environmental and scientific bay and Chapter 5 Starting points).

Fixed equipment

Many settings have fixed equipment, that is equipment attached to the ground and which cannot be moved. The difficulty with this type of equipment is that it can be limiting in helping children to learn. There are only a finite number of movements that can be made on it and it cannot be moved, changed or adapted to suit children's interests. After a while children actually become bored by the equipment and can use it less and less. Beautifully designed fixed equipment can stretch the designer's imagination, but can do little for a child's. Sometimes a fixed piece of equipment can become a magnet for poor behaviour.

What can you do?

* If you have fixed equipment do not just leave it, but try to make it different, add to it, change it. For example:

  The wooden house – make sure this is well resourced. Change the focus regularly as you would any imaginative play area. It could be a florist, a railway station, a shop counter or music corner (see Figure 3.53).

  Climbing apparatus – use it to attach equipment for the movement of water, such as guttering, pipes and tubing. Make it into a den using material and ropes (see Figure 3.9).

* Consider attaching A-frames, planks or material to fixed climbing equipment. It may be that you will need to find a home-made source of planks as the rungs on fixed climbing apparatus can be wider than the average plank hook up.

* It may be that you need to actually remove the fixed piece of equipment or part of it. I can think of a setting who realised that just one part of the climbing apparatus was problematic and had it removed and the play changed.

In and out available simultaneously

Outside and inside need to be available at the same time, so children can move freely between the two areas. Stevens (2003) found that practitioners found it difficult to understand what 'equal access' meant. She concluded that the word 'simultaneously' was a more useful term, meaning that at any time there was free play inside, and outside should be available alongside.

Having all the children outside at once, for a timetabled play, causes the following problems:

- Little or no planning goes into the area.

- A few or the same toys are put out day after day.

- Children tend to run around, very unfocused and 'manic'.

- Disagreements occur between children about the few toys that are available.

- Staff deal with disputes, and never teach a child so the only things that are learned are things the children teach themselves.

- Children behave in the same way every day.

- Some children dominate the area.

- Some children are scared of being outside.

- Staff do not enjoy being outside; they see it as a time for a break and a chat and to survive.

- Children can behave quite badly and can become bored.

- Children do not learn to concentrate, persevere or think.

This is not good education and I am almost inclined to say that it's not worth going out if this is the scenario. However, it is possible to change things by making outdoor play available at the same time as indoor play, planning it well and involving adults in high quality interactions. When out and in are simultaneously available there is a huge difference in behaviour, approach and learning. Children are not manic; they are purposeful in their play, considerate of others, less frenetic, wanting to learn, playing with different children and learning much more.

Case study
Sasha's experience, Jack and Jill's Playgroup

'In the setting where I work we had quite a structured timetable, consisting of free play from 9 to 10 a.m., where children chose the activity they would like to play with, then small group focused activity and snacktime from 10 to 11 a.m., where the children came together in their keygroups with their keyworker and played a game or an activity of their choice and had a snack. Outdoor play was from 11 to 11.30 a.m., weather permitting, or the children would use a large hall, which is available in bad weather. The problem we found was that boys in free play would want to race around chasing each other and we found it difficult to engage them in any meaningful play. If they played a game they would tend to want to play their game in their own group of boys and after a short period of time would seem uninterested and get bored and want to move away. They tended to stick together preferring to play with other boys and were uninterested in girls. When girls approached their play they would split into small groups and break from their play to play alone elsewhere. The keygroups are mixed so, at focused time, that would be the only time they would engage in play with the opposite sex.

'After attending the outdoor play workshop, the idea was to change the structure of the group, linking outdoor and indoor play. A few examples are taking the shop outside, building and construction and tables and chairs. There were creative activities as well as the wall for painting or chalking.

'We found the boys' behaviour to change quite dramatically when playing outside and instead of running around in their little groups playing tag or "policemen", they engaged in play with all peers, playing with equipment that they seemed to ignore or were uninterested in when inside playgroup, for example the dolls' house, games, drawing and painting at tables and painting the walls. In the warmer weather a range of equipment was used outside (the children are involved in choosing the equipment that they would like to play with). A bookcase was set up outside and the children enjoyed sitting looking at books for quite long periods of time. Whole-group storytime was outside and the boys would sit and listen, recalling storylines and suggesting an ending to the story, rather than when it was inside becoming fidgety and distracted. Boys seemed to be reluctant to join in with songs and rhymes, so again this was changed and the children took chairs outside to sit on and sing "Wheels on the Bus" and "Row the Boat". With this they were more active and seemed to enjoy songs and rhymes, often suggesting songs we could sing.

'When writing our curriculum plans outdoor play is linked with indoor play, so umbrellas and wellington boots have been purchased and a wide range of equipment has been collected so that the children can use the outside in all weathers.

'We have always taken the children on outings outside of playgroup, to the local shops to buy the fruit and cooking materials for the week, visits to the park, local library, train and bus station. Before the change of structure to the group this would be the only time when they would seem actively involved in conversation with all peers. After changing the structure of the group it has been found that boys' behaviour has changed. They no longer wander around in packs together. They tend to play with all peers and will engage for long periods of time in an activity or game, something that did not happen inside. The change in our setting has made an improvement in the group as a whole and boys and girls play harmoniously together.

'The benefit of the outdoor play workshop has been that many people attended from different settings and I came away with so many different ideas to use for our setting that will benefit my playgroup and offer all children the opportunity to learn and play in the environment that they feel more comfortable in.'

Suggested improvements

* To ensure that both indoor play and out are used well and neither disturbs the other, outside should be available as soon as possible after the children come to the setting. Do not use outdoor play as a carrot for being good during the rest of the session.

Case study

In a nursery school the children were able to go out for over an hour, free flowing between in and out. However, this was not until the children had been inside for about 40 minutes. About 10 minutes before the doors were opened some children started to move about the room, clearly not doing anything particular. Then more children joined in and the feeling in the room became one of anticipation and unrest. I was disturbed by this movement, as clearly were other children. Finally one of the children who had got up initially said: 'Can we go out?', to which the reply was: 'No, not yet, it's not quite time.' By the time the doors were opened the majority of the children had been disturbed. These children could not tell the time and yet they could feel amounts of time. They were unable to concentrate, waiting for outdoor play to happen.

* It is difficult to put a time limit on how long children should be outside. However, generally there needs to be at least an hour's play outside to ensure children have time to follow their interests, learn to concentrate and persevere and teaching plans can be carried out. It needs to be available whenever free flow indoor play is offered.

* If outside has to be timetabled and cannot be alongside indoor play then make sure that:

  it happens at the beginning of the session

  you are outside for as long as possible

  you incorporate outside into the plans

  it is well resourced and equipped

  adults work and play with the children.

Combining play outside and in

Outside and in need to be available at the same time so that children can move between the two. One way of achieving this is to link activities in and out.

Suggestions

* You could have a sorting office outside and a post office inside; a launderette inside and a washing line outside; a florist inside and a garden centre outside; a café outside and a house inside; a garage receptionist inside and the workshop outside. Of course all these imaginative areas could be outside, but having one in and one out gives children the opportunity to link the two areas themselves.

* Children can be encouraged to make objects at the technology table inside to use in their play outside. Children do not need fancy bought signs, menus,

Figure 4.10 Children making a gate using tape, scissors and glue from inside

binoculars, computers or flowers, all of these things can be made by the children (see Figure 2.38 where the boys made their own warning signs not to touch the toadstools).

* Although children will have resources to be used outside placed outside, they should also be able to access resources inside. It may be they want to play with a particular game outside, which is usually stored in the classroom. Unless there is a practical difficulty, such as it may blow away, children should see the outside as much as a workshop as inside and that resources can be used in either area (see Figure 4.10).

* Involve the children in talking about outside and how it can be used. Let them participate in setting up equipment outside – they will be very imaginative in what can be used effectively outside. We can become very narrow in our thoughts; children tend not to have such blocks.

Layout

Make sure the space is divided into areas, not rigidly, but flexibly, through the arrangement of resources and equipment or a chalk line. Create exploratory and enclosed areas using shrubs and trees (see Figure 4.11). Keep branches low so children have to bend down and creep, as these are useful motor skills. This is also a way of creating a quiet bay or an area for imaginative play.

Suggestions

* Get children involved in class and school projects, so they can discuss what they would like and physically help. For example making a water feature, creating a wild area, planting up shrubs, adding bark-chippings and top soil.

* Think about creating a hill or tree house, as children can feel safe high up and it gives a very different visual perspective.

* Rather than have a bike track, have a pedestrian path. The path shown in Figure 4.12 was made from brick, safety surface, half logs, pebbles, Astroturf, bark chippings and large stones. Children enjoy balancing on the different textures and it made one want to explore the far reaches of the garden.

Figure 4.11 Being somewhere else

Questions

Do you talk to parents about the value of outdoor play?

Do you see rain as a problem or just another weather feature?

What do you need to do to the environment to make sure all children have equality of opportunity and access?

Is the fixed equipment a magnet for poor or stereotypical behaviour?

Is the fixed equipment planned for? Do you use it in different ways?

Do children really have access (and know they do) to a whole host of resources and equipment?

Figure 4.12 Children enjoy this path of different textures

Chapter 5
Where do we go from here?

In this chapter I will be looking at how to make changes or develop the outdoor area, by sharing a number of ideas already put into practice.

Case study

Hertfordshire Local Education Authority decided to set up an outdoor curriculum project to run from May 2002 to January 2003. The 12 schools selected to participate in the project had already submitted their development plan identifying outdoor provision as a priority. The aim of the project was 'to support teachers in the development of good practice regarding the curriculum and outdoor play'. Schools had an initial input from myself, and site visits. The LEA supported them with documentation, networking and visits and the University of Cambridge provided academic rigour and focus, as this was to be an accredited course if

Figure 5.1 Carrying a cardboard box together – success, confidence and happiness

participants so wished. There was a range of schools involved: large, small, rural, urban and mixed age, all with differing needs.

The project was met with a high degree of commitment, enthusiasm, good humour, great ideas and imagination. All the schools developed, some more than others, and felt the project had been worthwhile and an incentive to achieve more than if the project had not been running. One school noted 'being involved in this project has been the catalyst for good practice for the whole of the Foundation Stage curriculum'. Very importantly children were positively affected by the changes. I picked up a number of general issues from the project, as follows.

*   Foundation Stage units have been created since the introduction of the *Curriculum Guidance for the Foundation Stage* (QCA 2000), combining nursery and reception or a number of reception classes, as well as the outdoor area. Some of the schools involved in the project had done this, but felt children could feel lost in a large outdoor area and many staff were inclined to supervise and not teach. Solutions were discussed such as partitioning off the garden area just outside each class, so each group still had their own outdoor space, but with the option of having free access to all, further into the garden area. Other suggestions included making sure each class group had their own imaginative bay and construction bay, but a shared environmental bay, or limiting the number of children outside so there was a manageable number outside.

*   Tracking children in a large outdoor area was considered problematic, but suggestions were made such as: naming those individuals to be observed; creating a running record for all children; and making sure all staff knew exactly what they were looking for when they observed children.

*   Overcoming the weather so children could go out all year round was considered important. A covered area, boxes of suitable clothing, not viewing wet weather as a problem and following

what a family would do in wet weather (which is go out but not be able to do the same things as when it is dry) were all seen as solutions.

*   Fencing and the positioning of the outdoor area was seen to be more important than initially realised and schools spent time considering the best positioning.

*   Improvements did not happen overnight, change took time. Children were gradually introduced to the change and were able to adapt to it.

Findings from the project

Funds can be found for outdoor play provision

This project seemed to demonstrate the saying, 'Where there is a will, there is a way.' Funding came from company donations, sponsorship, parental donations and help and school and PTA funds.

Children are different outside

Many of the staff found that improvements to the outdoor provision brought improvements for children: they were less inhibited, more relaxed, able to concentrate on activities for longer, more confident, able to plan their outdoor play and able to talk more freely. One child said 'I like doing shows outside, because I don't have to be quiet.'

Outdoor provision is for nursery and reception children

Outside wasn't seen as the domain of just nursery children and had the potential of being of positive benefit to all ages of children. One primary school was looking to make outdoor provision available to all ages. Another had created a 'green room' outside, a quiet and shady space for all age children to access.

A mound and slope can be used in many ways

One school needed something fairly vandal proof, so came up with the idea of a one metre mound, with a gentle slope on one side and a steeper slope on the other side. Rubble and rubbish from a local building site was used, plus top soil, water-retaining granules and very tough grass seed. Children were involved in the construction and care of the mound. It has been used for: physical development such as running and rolling over and round; mathematical development including measuring over and around; and creative development by sketching it throughout the seasons. The staff have been amazed at how much it has been used.

The use of materials can be imaginative

Materials were found which were not too costly and there were resources outside that were not being used at all. For example:

Three tractor tyres were used to hold bark, compost and gravel for children to use for digging and transporting. Each tyre had a cover to keep the contents clean.

Fencing was used for threading and weaving.

Trees were used for motor skill development by hanging objects from them such as plastic bottles

to aim balls at and hoops to aim balls through. They were also used for musical development by hanging bottles containing various materials that could be tapped producing a variety of sounds.

The whole staff group, governors and parents needed to be involved

Schools found they had to educate parents and allay their worries. Once they saw outdoor play working parents were reassured. Parents commented that their children seemed much happier, there was more going on in the classrooms, and the work in school seemed more magical since the project began. One school made sure the governors were fully involved with the project and this helped bring parents on board.

Figure 5.2 Writing to a friend outside

Topic/project/curriculum boxes can be made

Many of the schools set up boxes to gather resources and this helped channel their thinking. For example one school set up a number box, a music/movement box and a creative/making box, each with a list of contents and learning objectives. They found that children's investigative skills improved through using these boxes of resources. Another school put together topic boxes with cards suggesting ideas for use.

Case study

Southmead Primary School (see also p. 12) has a combined nursery and reception unit, offering a play-based curriculum. The day runs from 9 a.m. until 3.30 p.m. with four group activities throughout the day, two in the morning and two in the afternoon, interspersed by four periods of free play (9.00–9.40 a.m., 10.05–11.25 a.m., 1.00–1.40 p.m. and 2.05–3.00 p.m.). What I found particularly noticeable outside was the calm atmosphere during the free

flow play: children were not aggressive, manic, or disruptive; rather, they were very able, interested and hard working. Transition from group to free play was easy, the quality of interactions between children was supportive and children appeared very close to and secure with the adults. During a period of rebuilding the unit had to move to the school hall, with a temporary outdoor area, and again the atmosphere was calm and productive.

The unit has now been running for two years and involves a high input from the staff before, during and after the children's day, but the children are considered to be happier, calmer, more focused and on task (see Figure 5.1) than when the more formal approach was being run. Since the unit has been running a more play-based curriculum the children seem to have a thirst for knowledge, seem ready to get down to writing and mathematical work and are thinkers (see Figures 5.2 and 5.3). Giving choice to children is seen as making sure they are motivated, curious and stimulated.

Figure 5.3 Writing about the tennis match

Rainy days

funnels
plastic bottles
tin trays
buckets
plastic tunnels
tubes
drain pipes
guttering
umbrella
paint
paint brushes (all sizes)
sheet of plastic
washing-up liquid
sponges, jugs, cloths for wiping up
brooms for sweeping puddles
magnifying glass
rainstick
water pump
water chute
rubber gloves with holes
assortment of objects to float – bottle tops, leaves, feathers, boats
assortment of objects to catch the rain – plastic cups, jugs, watering can
pattern makers, e.g. bike tyres
chalks

Books

Fiction

By Shirley Hughes:

Alfie's Feet, Hutchinson Children's Books

An Evening at Alfie's, Red Fox

Out and About Through the Years, Walker Books

Non-fiction

Watching the Weather, Heinemann 1st Library

Rhymes and songs

Rainsong, Snowsong, Philemon Sturgess, North South Books

Action Rhymes, Compiled by John Foster and illustrated by Carol Thompson, Oxford University Press

Don't Worry Grandpa, Nick Ward, Red Fox

Nursery Rhymes – 'Dr Fosters', 'It's Raining It's Pouring', 'I Hear Thunder'

Added to this...

Waterwheels? How can we show the power of heavy rain?

Water pathways – exploring channels for water, e.g. natural (mud, sand etc.) and man-made (plastic tubing, sheeting etc.)

Take a photo of very heavy rain and put on to overhead transparency sheet. Project the image on to a screen/wall and accompany with suitable music on days when the weather is extreme and outdoor provision has to be restricted.

Print with puddles and mud!... 'We're going on a bear hunt...'

Figure 5.4 Some ideas for the rain box (Source: from Karen Musgrove, Essex County Council)

Starting points

One of my suggestions for the adult role is offering starting points to children, but often adults need starting points themselves. An effective starting point is making up boxes of resources. These may be curriculum, topic, project, learning bay or feature based. At an early years conference in Essex 'The Classroom Without a Roof' in November 2002, the weather box theme was used to encourage delegates to think what they would put into the weather boxes for rain, snow, wind and sun (see Figure 5.4). People were asked to consider both free and found materials, as well as those that were commercially made.
The delegates were extremely inventive, for example from the simple plastic bottle came a multitude of ideas, three of which were:

* Filling it with water to spray at walls to demonstrate how a thin line may dry in the sun.

* Filling it with water and spraying out on a windy day to see how the spray may be blown and how far.

* Making a funnel to collect snow by cutting two-thirds the way up the bottle and placing this upside down in the rest of the bottle and using this apparatus to measure the snow's melting time.

These are three ideas from free materials, but you need the time to think about more ideas, write them down and collect the resources. The list can always be added to but then you are always ready to utilise the weather feature when it occurs.

Making changes

To develop or change the outside area takes a good deal of discussion and consideration before action. Where you start will depend on where you are at the moment. It could be: collecting resources into named boxes; assessing adult behaviour; getting rid of resources and gathering more versatile materials; or changing the timing of outdoor play. Changes need to be manageable and measurable.

Outdoor play is for all ages and it is heartening to see Key Stage 1 and 2 schools wanting to develop outdoor play for their children. Figure 5.5 shows how a climbing frame, a metal pole and brush for the oars, bags, pads, telephones and long dresses have transported two six and a half-year-olds into the middle of the Atlantic. These children gathered resources, negotiated the direction of play and then immersed themselves in their imaginations.

Figure 5.5 Two six and a half-year-olds enjoying the benefits of outdoor play

Resources and contacts

Books and activity packs

* CAMERON, J. (1993) *'Mummy I'm Bored!'*. London: Anderson Press.

  This is a book for inspiring you with ideas for how to change cardboard boxes. Some of the ideas are too adult led, but can be adapted by children to make themselves.

* CARTWRIGHT, P., SCOTT, K. and STEVENS, J. (2002) *A Place to Learn*. London: PDA Design and Advertising.

  A very accessible pack about all aspects of Foundation Stage teaching and learning.

* FEATHERSTONE, S. (2003) *The Little Book of Outside in All Weathers*. Leicestershire: Featherstone Education.

  I like this Little Book (the trademark name for this series) basically because Sally Featherstone celebrates the rain and wet weather!

* NICHOLSON, R. (2003) *Ideas for Foundation Stage Learning*. London: Wandsworth Borough Council.

  This is a very accessible pack of activities for both inside and outside. I like the way Rob Nicholson, the author, has put all the outdoor play ideas first in the listings.

Equipment

* Brian Clegg, Slackcote Mill, Slackcote Lane, Delph, Oldham OL3 5TP

  Tel: 01457 785881

  Suppliers of A-frames, ladders, trucks, pushchairs and storage trolleys.

* Charity shops and parental contributions. Help parents to appreciate the value of outdoor play and they will help with supplying resources.

* Community Playthings, Robertsbridge, East Sussex TN32 5DR

  Tel: 0800 387457 www.communityplaythings.com

  A supplier of well-made and long lasting equipment for all aspects of play. In particular playcubes, carriages, wheelbarrows and blocks (unit and hollow, Figures 2.20 and 2.36).

* DIY and furniture stores have very useful materials. It is often a case of just wandering through them and being inspired.

* Galt Educational, Johnsonbrook Road, Hyde, Cheshire SK14 4QT

  Tel: 08702 424477 enquiries@galt-educational.co.uk

  Suppliers of trolleys, mats, plastic cushions, climbing trestles, ladders, cubes, barrels, circle carts, trucks/ wagons, balls and hoops and blocks as in Figure 3.13.

* GLS Educational Supplies Limited

  Tel: 020 8805 8333 sales@glsed.co.uk

  Suppliers of A-frames, ladders, planks and bars.

* Mindstretchers, The Warehouse, Rossie Place, Auchterarder, Perthshire PH3 1AJ

  Tel: 01764 664409 enquiries@mindstretchers.co.uk

  I liked the bags they make up to use outside, so that children are equipped with a collection of objects to use imaginatively.

* NES Arnold, Novara House, Excelsior Road, Ashby Park, Ashby de la Zouch, Leicestershire LE65 1NG

  Tel: 0870 6000 192 www.nesarnold.co.uk

  Suppliers of A-frames, ladders, planks, poles, parallel bars, hay carts and mats.

* Treeblocks (Figure 3.14)

  Tel: 800 873 4960 www.treeblocks.com

  I thought these blocks were very appealing.

* Trucks (Figures 3.2 and 3.3)

  Contact Helen Bilton helenbilton@btinternet.com Tel: 0118 9261537 hob2@tutor.open.ac.uk for details and sales.

* WESCO, 114 Highfield Road, Wilham, Essex CM8 2HH

  Tel: 01376 503590 www.wesco-group.com

  Suppliers of ropes, balancing ropes, motor education kits and balls.

Advice

* Learning through Landscapes (LTL), Third Floor, Southside Offices, The Law Courts, Winchester SO23 9DL

  Tel: 01962 846258 schoolgrounds-uk@ltl.org.uk

  This is the National School Grounds charity, which can advise on grounds and funding and provide legal and technical advice. They produce books and pamphlets. Their work deals with all school age groups.

Bibliography

ADAMS, E. (2003) 'Smart squiggles', *Guardian Education* 15 July, 4–5.

ARMSTRONG, N. (1996) *New Directions in Physical Education*. London: Cassell.

BATES, B. (1986) 'Like rats in a rage', *Times Educational Supplement* **2**, 20 September, 11.

BILTON, H. (2004) 'Promoting physical development', Study Topic 12, from Open University course materials E124 'Supporting children's learning in the early years'. Milton Keynes: The Open University.

CURTIS, P. (2003) 'Young guns', *Guardian* (Education section), 16 September, 24.

DEPARTMENT OF EDUCATION AND SCIENCE (DES) (1989) *Aspects of Primary Education. The education of children under five*. London: HMSO.

DUNNE, E. and BENNETT, N. (2003) *Teaching and Learning in Groups*. London: Routledge Falmer.

EDGINGTON, M. (2003) *The Great Outdoors. Developing children's learning through outdoor provision*, 2nd edn. London: British Association for Early Childhood Education.

EDWARDS, R. AND FEE, E. (2003) *Outdoor Learning. Developing provision in Early Years settings*. Gloucestershire: Gloucestershire County Council.

HARDING, S. (2002) 'What's happening with the bikes?', Action research assignment in part fulfilment of MA Education and Care, London: University of North London/Pen Green Centre for Under-fives and their Families.

HAWORTH, J., DESFORGES, A. and ORGILL, D. (1992) 'Home sweet home corner', *Education 3–13*, 37–42.

McLEAN, S. V. (1991) *The Human Encounter: Teachers and children living together in preschools*. London: Falmer Press.

NICHOLSON, R. (2001) *Planning for Foundation Stage Learning* London: Wandsworth Borough Council.

NICHOLSON, R. (2003) 'All about planning', *Nursery World* 6 March, 15–22.

NORTHEN, S. (2003) 'Play', *Times Educational Supplement* 2 May, 13–16. Details of the research by Professors Siraj-Blatchford and Sylva into 'shared sustained thinking' are on the DfES website (www.dfes.gov.uk).

OUVRY, M. (2000) *Exercising Muscles and Minds. Outdoor play and the early years curriculum*. London: The National Early Years Network.

QUALIFICATION AND CURRICULUM AUTHORITY (QCA) (2000) *Curriculum Guidance for the Foundation Stage*. London: QCA.

SHAW, M. (2003) 'Ways through laddish culture', *Times Educational Supplement* 11 July, 8.

STEPHENSON, A. (2003) 'Physical risk-taking: dangerous or endangered?', *Early Years* **23**(1), 35–43.

STEVENS, V. (2003) 'The developing child and the Early Years curriculum', dissertation in part fulfillment of BA Education, University of Nottingham Trent.